50 Mexican Restaurant Dessert Recipes for Home

By: Kelly Johnson

Table of Contents

- Chicken Enchiladas
- Beef Tacos
- Fish Tacos
- Chicken Quesadillas
- Barbacoa Beef Burritos
- Carnitas Tacos
- Cheese Enchiladas
- Pork Tamales
- Chimichangas
- Shrimp Ceviche
- Chicken Tortilla Soup
- Mexican Street Corn (Elote)
- Chile Rellenos
- Beef Fajitas
- Chicken Fajitas
- Huevos Rancheros
- Pork Pozole
- Sopes
- Mexican Rice
- Refried Beans
- Tostadas
- Baja Fish Tacos
- Chicken Tostadas
- Beef Taquitos
- Chili Con Carne
- Mexican Stuffed Peppers
- Burrito Bowls
- Green Chile Chicken Enchiladas
- Mexican Chilaquiles
- Beef and Bean Burritos
- Chicken and Cheese Nachos
- Mexican Meatballs (Albondigas)

- Spicy Pork Carnitas
- Black Bean Soup
- Pico de Gallo
- Guacamole
- Chicken Mole
- Vegetarian Enchiladas
- Queso Fundido
- Mexican Pizza
- Beef Tostadas
- Chicken Taquitos
- Tex-Mex Chicken Salad
- Mexican Stuffed Shells
- Pork and Pineapple Tacos
- Chili Verde
- Chicken and Spinach Enchiladas
- Shrimp Tacos with Cilantro Lime Sauce
- Bacon-Wrapped Jalapeno Poppers
- Mexican Bean Salad

Chicken Enchiladas

Ingredients:

For the Chicken Filling:

- **Chicken Breasts:** 2 large, boneless and skinless
- **Olive Oil:** 1 tbsp
- **Onion:** 1/2, finely chopped
- **Garlic:** 2 cloves, minced
- **Ground Cumin:** 1 tsp
- **Chili Powder:** 1 tsp
- **Paprika:** 1/2 tsp
- **Salt:** 1/2 tsp
- **Black Pepper:** 1/4 tsp
- **Cilantro:** 1/4 cup, chopped (optional)
- **Cheddar Cheese:** 1 cup, shredded (or Mexican blend cheese)

For the Enchiladas:

- **Corn or Flour Tortillas:** 8 (6-inch or 8-inch size)
- **Enchilada Sauce:** 2 cups (store-bought or homemade)
- **Cheddar or Mexican Blend Cheese:** 1 1/2 cups, shredded (for topping)

For Garnish (optional):

- **Fresh Cilantro:** Chopped
- **Sour Cream**
- **Chopped Green Onions**
- **Sliced Jalapeños**
- **Sliced Black Olives**

Instructions:

1. **Prepare the Chicken Filling:**
    - **Cook the Chicken:** Preheat your oven to 375°F (190°C). Heat olive oil in a skillet over medium heat. Add the chicken breasts and cook for 6-8 minutes per side, or until cooked through. Remove from the skillet and let cool slightly. Shred the chicken using two forks or chop into small pieces.
    - **Cook Aromatics:** In the same skillet, add the chopped onion and cook until softened, about 3-4 minutes. Add the minced garlic and cook for another minute.
    - **Combine:** Return the shredded chicken to the skillet. Stir in cumin, chili powder, paprika, salt, and black pepper. Cook for 2-3 minutes to allow the flavors to meld. Stir in the chopped cilantro if using. Remove from heat.

2. **Prepare the Enchiladas:**
   - **Warm Tortillas:** Heat the tortillas in a dry skillet or microwave to make them more pliable.
   - **Fill Tortillas:** Spread a small amount of enchilada sauce on the bottom of a baking dish. Place a portion of the chicken filling and a sprinkle of cheese in the center of each tortilla. Roll up the tortillas and place them seam-side down in the baking dish.
3. **Assemble and Bake:**
   - **Top with Sauce and Cheese:** Pour the remaining enchilada sauce over the rolled tortillas, ensuring they are well covered. Sprinkle the top with shredded cheese.
   - **Bake:** Cover with foil and bake in the preheated oven for 20 minutes. Remove the foil and bake for an additional 10-15 minutes, or until the cheese is melted and bubbly, and the enchiladas are heated through.
4. **Serve:**
   - **Garnish:** Remove from the oven and let cool for a few minutes. Garnish with fresh cilantro, sour cream, chopped green onions, sliced jalapeños, or sliced black olives if desired.
   - **Enjoy:** Serve hot with your favorite Mexican sides, such as Mexican rice or refried beans.

Tips:

- **For extra flavor:** Add a layer of cooked onions or bell peppers to the filling.
- **For a spicier kick:** Use a spicy enchilada sauce or add a dash of hot sauce to the filling.
- **Make ahead:** You can assemble the enchiladas ahead of time and refrigerate or freeze them before baking. Just bake them straight from the fridge or freezer, adjusting the cooking time as needed.

These Chicken Enchiladas are a hearty and flavorful meal that's perfect for family dinners or gatherings. Enjoy!

Beef Tacos

Ingredients:

For the Beef Filling:

- **Ground Beef:** 1 lb
- **Olive Oil:** 1 tbsp (optional, for cooking)
- **Onion:** 1/2, finely chopped
- **Garlic:** 2 cloves, minced
- **Chili Powder:** 2 tbsp
- **Ground Cumin:** 1 tsp
- **Paprika:** 1 tsp
- **Oregano:** 1/2 tsp
- **Salt:** 1 tsp
- **Black Pepper:** 1/2 tsp
- **Tomato Paste:** 2 tbsp
- **Beef Broth:** 1/2 cup (or water)
- **Red Pepper Flakes:** 1/4 tsp (optional, for heat)

For the Tacos:

- **Taco Shells or Tortillas:** 8 (soft flour or corn tortillas, or hard taco shells)
- **Shredded Lettuce:** 1 cup
- **Diced Tomatoes:** 1 cup
- **Shredded Cheese:** 1 cup (cheddar, Mexican blend, or your choice)
- **Sour Cream:** 1/2 cup
- **Salsa:** 1/2 cup
- **Chopped Fresh Cilantro:** 1/4 cup
- **Lime Wedges:** For serving

Instructions:

1. **Cook the Beef Filling:**
    - **Brown the Beef:** In a large skillet, heat olive oil over medium-high heat (if using). Add the ground beef and cook, breaking it up with a spoon, until browned and fully cooked, about 5-7 minutes. Drain any excess fat.
    - **Add Aromatics:** Add the chopped onion and cook for 3-4 minutes, or until softened. Stir in the minced garlic and cook for another minute.
    - **Season:** Add the chili powder, ground cumin, paprika, oregano, salt, and black pepper. Stir well to coat the beef with the spices.
    - **Add Tomato Paste and Broth:** Stir in the tomato paste and cook for 1-2 minutes. Add the beef broth (or water) and red pepper flakes (if using). Simmer

for 5-7 minutes, or until the liquid has reduced and the mixture is thickened. Adjust seasoning if needed.
2. **Prepare the Tacos:**
   - **Warm Taco Shells/Tortillas:** If using soft tortillas, warm them in a dry skillet over medium heat or in the microwave. For hard taco shells, follow package instructions to crisp them up.
   - **Assemble Tacos:** Spoon the beef mixture into the taco shells or tortillas. Top with shredded lettuce, diced tomatoes, shredded cheese, sour cream, and salsa.
3. **Garnish and Serve:**
   - **Garnish:** Sprinkle with chopped fresh cilantro and serve with lime wedges on the side for a fresh burst of flavor.
   - **Serve:** Enjoy immediately while the tacos are warm.

Tips:

- **For extra flavor:** Add a squeeze of lime juice over the beef mixture before serving.
- **For a spicier kick:** Incorporate chopped jalapeños or a dash of hot sauce into the beef mixture.
- **Make it a meal:** Serve with Mexican rice, refried beans, or a side salad for a complete meal.

Beef Tacos are a versatile and delicious option for any meal, offering a great balance of flavors and textures. Enjoy your homemade tacos!

Fish Tacos

Ingredients:

For the Fish:

- **White Fish Filets:** 1 lb (such as cod, tilapia, or halibut)
- **All-Purpose Flour:** 1 cup
- **Cornstarch:** 1/4 cup
- **Paprika:** 1 tsp
- **Ground Cumin:** 1/2 tsp
- **Garlic Powder:** 1/2 tsp
- **Onion Powder:** 1/2 tsp
- **Salt:** 1/2 tsp
- **Black Pepper:** 1/4 tsp
- **Egg:** 1, beaten
- **Buttermilk:** 1/2 cup
- **Vegetable Oil:** For frying (about 1/2 cup)

For the Slaw:

- **Shredded Cabbage:** 2 cups (green or red cabbage, or a mix)
- **Carrot:** 1 large, shredded
- **Fresh Cilantro:** 1/4 cup, chopped
- **Lime Juice:** 2 tbsp
- **Mayonnaise:** 1/4 cup
- **Honey:** 1 tbsp
- **Salt:** 1/4 tsp
- **Black Pepper:** 1/4 tsp

For Serving:

- **Taco Shells or Tortillas:** 8 (soft flour or corn tortillas, or hard taco shells)
- **Fresh Cilantro:** Chopped, for garnish
- **Lime Wedges:** For serving
- **Avocado Slices:** Optional
- **Salsa or Pico de Gallo:** Optional

Instructions:

1. **Prepare the Fish:**
    - **Cut and Season:** Cut the fish filets into bite-sized strips. In a shallow dish, combine flour, cornstarch, paprika, cumin, garlic powder, onion powder, salt, and black pepper.

- **Dredge Fish:** Dip each piece of fish first into the beaten egg, then into the flour mixture, coating well.
- **Heat Oil:** Heat vegetable oil in a large skillet over medium-high heat. Test the oil temperature by dropping a small piece of flour into the oil; it should sizzle.
- **Fry Fish:** Fry the coated fish pieces in batches until golden brown and crispy, about 3-4 minutes per side. Remove from the skillet and drain on paper towels. Keep warm.

2. **Prepare the Slaw:**
   - **Combine Ingredients:** In a large bowl, mix shredded cabbage, shredded carrot, and chopped cilantro.
   - **Make Dressing:** In a small bowl, whisk together lime juice, mayonnaise, honey, salt, and black pepper.
   - **Toss Slaw:** Pour the dressing over the cabbage mixture and toss to combine. Set aside.

3. **Assemble the Tacos:**
   - **Warm Tortillas/Shells:** Warm the tortillas in a dry skillet over medium heat or in the microwave. If using hard taco shells, follow package instructions to heat them.
   - **Fill Tacos:** Place a few pieces of crispy fish in each tortilla or shell. Top with a generous amount of the slaw.

4. **Garnish and Serve:**
   - **Garnish:** Sprinkle with additional chopped fresh cilantro and serve with lime wedges on the side.
   - **Optional:** Add avocado slices and/or salsa or pico de gallo if desired.

Tips:

- **For extra flavor:** Add a sprinkle of chili powder or a drizzle of hot sauce to the fish before serving.
- **For a lighter version:** Use grilled or baked fish instead of fried.
- **To make ahead:** Prepare the slaw a few hours in advance and store it in the refrigerator to let the flavors meld.

Fish Tacos are a fresh and vibrant dish that's both satisfying and versatile. Enjoy these flavorful tacos with your favorite sides for a perfect meal!

Chicken Quesadillas

Ingredients:

For the Chicken Filling:

- **Chicken Breasts:** 2 large, boneless and skinless
- **Olive Oil:** 1 tbsp
- **Onion:** 1/2, finely chopped
- **Garlic:** 2 cloves, minced
- **Ground Cumin:** 1/2 tsp
- **Chili Powder:** 1 tsp
- **Paprika:** 1/2 tsp
- **Salt:** 1/2 tsp
- **Black Pepper:** 1/4 tsp
- **Cilantro:** 1/4 cup, chopped (optional)

For the Quesadillas:

- **Flour Tortillas:** 4 (10-inch size, or smaller if preferred)
- **Shredded Cheddar Cheese:** 1 cup
- **Shredded Monterey Jack Cheese:** 1 cup (or use Mexican blend cheese)
- **Butter or Oil:** 2 tbsp (for cooking)
- **Sour Cream:** For serving (optional)
- **Salsa or Pico de Gallo:** For serving (optional)

Instructions:

1. **Prepare the Chicken Filling:**
   - **Cook the Chicken:** Heat olive oil in a skillet over medium heat. Add the chicken breasts and cook for about 6-8 minutes per side, or until fully cooked (internal temperature should reach 165°F or 75°C). Remove from the skillet and let cool slightly.
   - **Shred the Chicken:** Once cooled, shred the chicken using two forks or chop into small pieces.
   - **Season and Sauté:** In the same skillet, add the chopped onion and cook until softened, about 3-4 minutes. Add the minced garlic and cook for another minute. Stir in the ground cumin, chili powder, paprika, salt, and black pepper. Add the shredded chicken and cook for 2-3 minutes, mixing well. Stir in chopped cilantro if desired. Remove from heat.
2. **Assemble the Quesadillas:**
   - **Prepare Tortillas:** Place one tortilla on a clean surface. Sprinkle half of the shredded cheese evenly over one half of the tortilla. Spread a portion of the

chicken filling over the cheese. Sprinkle the remaining cheese on top of the chicken and fold the tortilla in half.
    - **Cook Quesadillas:** Heat a large skillet or griddle over medium heat and add a small amount of butter or oil. Place the folded tortilla in the skillet and cook for 2-3 minutes per side, or until golden brown and the cheese is melted. Repeat with the remaining tortillas.
3. **Serve:**
    - **Cut and Serve:** Remove the quesadillas from the skillet and let them cool for a minute. Cut into wedges and serve with sour cream and salsa or pico de gallo if desired.

Tips:

- **For extra flavor:** Add additional ingredients to the filling, such as sautéed bell peppers, mushrooms, or black beans.
- **For a spicier kick:** Mix in some chopped jalapeños or a sprinkle of red pepper flakes.
- **To make ahead:** Prepare the chicken filling in advance and store it in the refrigerator for up to 3 days. Assemble and cook the quesadillas when ready to serve.

Chicken Quesadillas are quick to make, customizable, and packed with flavor. Enjoy them as a satisfying lunch or dinner option!

Barbacoa Beef Burritos

Ingredients:

For the Barbacoa Beef:

- **Beef Chuck Roast:** 3 lbs, trimmed and cut into large chunks
- **Olive Oil:** 2 tbsp
- **Onion:** 1, chopped
- **Garlic:** 4 cloves, minced
- **Chipotle Peppers in Adobo Sauce:** 2-3 peppers (from a can), chopped
- **Adobo Sauce:** 2 tbsp (from the can of chipotle peppers)
- **Ground Cumin:** 1 tbsp
- **Ground Oregano:** 1 tbsp
- **Paprika:** 1 tbsp
- **Ground Coriander:** 1 tsp
- **Ground Black Pepper:** 1/2 tsp
- **Salt:** 1 tsp
- **Beef Broth:** 1 cup
- **Lime Juice:** 2 tbsp
- **Bay Leaves:** 2

For the Burritos:

- **Flour Tortillas:** 8 (10-inch size)
- **Cooked Rice:** 2 cups
- **Refried Beans:** 1 cup
- **Shredded Cheese:** 1 1/2 cups (cheddar, Monterey Jack, or Mexican blend)
- **Shredded Lettuce:** 1 cup
- **Diced Tomatoes:** 1 cup
- **Sour Cream:** 1/2 cup
- **Fresh Cilantro:** Chopped, for garnish
- **Salsa or Pico de Gallo:** For serving

Instructions:

1. **Prepare the Barbacoa Beef:**
    - **Sear the Beef:** In a large skillet, heat olive oil over medium-high heat. Add the beef chunks and sear until browned on all sides, about 5-7 minutes. Remove the beef from the skillet and set aside.
    - **Cook Aromatics:** In the same skillet, add chopped onion and cook until softened, about 3-4 minutes. Stir in minced garlic and cook for another minute.
    - **Combine Ingredients:** In a slow cooker or pressure cooker, combine the seared beef, cooked onions and garlic, chopped chipotle peppers, adobo sauce, ground

cumin, ground oregano, paprika, ground coriander, black pepper, salt, beef broth, lime juice, and bay leaves.
    - **Cook:** For slow cooking, cover and cook on low for 8 hours or until the beef is tender and shreds easily. For a pressure cooker or Instant Pot, cook on high pressure for 60 minutes and let the pressure release naturally.
    - **Shred Beef:** Once cooked, remove the beef from the slow cooker or pressure cooker. Shred the beef with two forks and return it to the cooking liquid. Stir to combine.
2. **Assemble the Burritos:**
    - **Warm Tortillas:** Heat the tortillas in a dry skillet over medium heat or in the microwave until warm and pliable.
    - **Fill Burritos:** Lay a tortilla flat on a clean surface. Spread a portion of refried beans down the center of the tortilla. Top with a portion of cooked rice, a generous amount of barbacoa beef, and shredded cheese.
    - **Fold and Roll:** Fold the sides of the tortilla over the filling and roll up from the bottom to form a burrito. Repeat with the remaining tortillas and filling.
3. **Serve:**
    - **Optional:** For extra crispy burritos, you can lightly pan-fry them in a skillet with a little oil until golden brown and crispy on both sides.
    - **Garnish and Enjoy:** Serve the burritos with shredded lettuce, diced tomatoes, sour cream, and fresh cilantro. Pair with salsa or pico de gallo on the side.

Tips:

- **For added flavor:** Include extras like sautéed bell peppers, onions, or avocado slices in the burritos.
- **Make it spicy:** Adjust the amount of chipotle peppers or add a dash of hot sauce if you prefer more heat.
- **Make ahead:** The barbacoa beef can be made ahead of time and stored in the refrigerator for up to 3 days or frozen for up to 3 months.

Barbacoa Beef Burritos are a delicious and hearty meal, packed with rich flavors and satisfying fillings. Enjoy!

Carnitas Tacos

Ingredients:

For the Carnitas:

- **Pork Shoulder (or Pork Butt):** 3 lbs, trimmed and cut into large chunks
- **Olive Oil:** 2 tbsp
- **Onion:** 1, chopped
- **Garlic:** 4 cloves, minced
- **Ground Cumin:** 1 tbsp
- **Chili Powder:** 2 tsp
- **Paprika:** 1 tsp
- **Dried Oregano:** 1 tsp
- **Ground Coriander:** 1 tsp
- **Salt:** 1 1/2 tsp
- **Black Pepper:** 1 tsp
- **Orange Juice:** 1 cup
- **Lime Juice:** 1/4 cup
- **Beef Broth:** 1 cup (or water)
- **Bay Leaves:** 2
- **Cilantro:** Chopped, for garnish

For the Tacos:

- **Corn or Flour Tortillas:** 8 (6-inch or 8-inch size)
- **Shredded Lettuce:** 1 cup
- **Diced Tomatoes:** 1 cup
- **Shredded Cheese:** 1 cup (cheddar, Mexican blend, or your choice)
- **Sour Cream:** 1/2 cup
- **Salsa or Pico de Gallo:** For serving
- **Lime Wedges:** For serving

Instructions:

1. **Prepare the Carnitas:**
   - **Sear the Pork:** Heat olive oil in a large skillet or Dutch oven over medium-high heat. Add the pork chunks and sear on all sides until browned, about 5-7 minutes. Remove the pork from the skillet and set aside.
   - **Cook Aromatics:** In the same skillet, add chopped onion and cook until softened, about 3-4 minutes. Stir in minced garlic and cook for another minute.
   - **Combine Ingredients:** Return the seared pork to the skillet. Add ground cumin, chili powder, paprika, dried oregano, ground coriander, salt, and black pepper. Stir to coat the pork with the spices.

- **Add Liquids:** Pour in the orange juice, lime juice, and beef broth. Add bay leaves. Bring to a simmer.
 - **Cook:** Cover and reduce heat to low. Cook for 2-3 hours, or until the pork is tender and shreds easily. Alternatively, cook in a slow cooker on low for 6-8 hours or on high for 4-5 hours. If using a pressure cooker or Instant Pot, cook on high pressure for 60 minutes and let the pressure release naturally.
2. **Crisp the Carnitas:**
 - **Shred the Pork:** Once cooked, remove the pork from the skillet or slow cooker. Shred the pork with two forks and discard any large pieces of fat. Return the shredded pork to the cooking liquid.
 - **Crisp the Pork:** To achieve crispy edges, heat a large skillet over medium-high heat. Add a small amount of the shredded pork to the hot skillet in a single layer. Let it cook without stirring for 3-4 minutes until it starts to crisp up. Stir and cook for an additional 2-3 minutes. Repeat with the remaining pork.
3. **Assemble the Tacos:**
 - **Warm Tortillas:** Heat the tortillas in a dry skillet over medium heat or in the microwave until warm and pliable.
 - **Fill Tacos:** Place a generous amount of crispy carnitas in each tortilla. Top with shredded lettuce, diced tomatoes, shredded cheese, and a dollop of sour cream.
4. **Serve:**
 - **Garnish:** Sprinkle with chopped fresh cilantro and serve with lime wedges on the side.
 - **Optional:** Add salsa or pico de gallo for extra flavor and freshness.

Tips:

- **For a smoky flavor:** Add a teaspoon of smoked paprika or a small amount of chipotle powder to the seasoning mix.
- **For added crunch:** Top with thinly sliced radishes or pickled onions.
- **Make ahead:** Carnitas can be made in advance and stored in the refrigerator for up to 3 days or frozen for up to 3 months. Reheat thoroughly before serving.

Carnitas Tacos are a delicious and versatile option, full of rich, savory flavor and perfect for a quick and satisfying meal. Enjoy!

Cheese Enchiladas

Ingredients:

For the Enchiladas:

- **Corn Tortillas:** 8 (6-inch or 8-inch size)
- **Shredded Cheddar Cheese:** 2 cups
- **Shredded Monterey Jack Cheese:** 1 cup (or Mexican blend cheese)
- **Olive Oil:** 2 tbsp (for softening tortillas)
- **Chopped Onion:** 1/2 cup (optional, for added flavor)
- **Chopped Fresh Cilantro:** For garnish (optional)

For the Enchilada Sauce:

- **Olive Oil:** 2 tbsp
- **Chopped Onion:** 1/2 cup
- **Garlic:** 2 cloves, minced
- **Chili Powder:** 2 tbsp
- **Ground Cumin:** 1 tsp
- **Paprika:** 1/2 tsp
- **Tomato Paste:** 2 tbsp
- **All-Purpose Flour:** 2 tbsp
- **Vegetable Broth:** 2 cups (or chicken broth)
- **Salt:** 1/2 tsp
- **Black Pepper:** 1/4 tsp

Instructions:

1. **Prepare the Enchilada Sauce:**
    - **Sauté Aromatics:** In a medium saucepan, heat olive oil over medium heat. Add the chopped onion and cook until softened, about 3-4 minutes. Stir in the minced garlic and cook for another minute.
    - **Add Spices and Paste:** Stir in the chili powder, ground cumin, paprika, and tomato paste. Cook for 1-2 minutes, stirring frequently.
    - **Make Sauce:** Sprinkle the flour over the onion mixture and cook for another minute, stirring constantly. Gradually whisk in the vegetable broth and bring the mixture to a simmer.
    - **Simmer and Season:** Let the sauce simmer for 10 minutes, or until it thickens slightly. Season with salt and black pepper. Remove from heat.
2. **Prepare the Tortillas:**
    - **Soften Tortillas:** Heat olive oil in a skillet over medium heat. Quickly fry each tortilla for about 10-15 seconds per side until they are softened but not crisp. Drain on paper towels.

3. **Assemble the Enchiladas:**
    - **Preheat Oven:** Preheat your oven to 375°F (190°C).
    - **Fill Tortillas:** Spread a small amount of enchilada sauce on the bottom of a baking dish. Place a generous amount of shredded cheese in the center of each tortilla. Roll up the tortilla and place seam-side down in the baking dish.
    - **Top with Sauce and Cheese:** Once all tortillas are in the dish, pour the remaining enchilada sauce over the top. Sprinkle additional shredded cheese over the sauce.
4. **Bake:**
    - **Bake:** Cover with foil and bake in the preheated oven for 20 minutes. Remove the foil and bake for an additional 10 minutes, or until the cheese is melted and bubbly.
5. **Serve:**
    - **Garnish:** Remove from the oven and let cool for a few minutes. Garnish with chopped fresh cilantro if desired.
    - **Enjoy:** Serve with your favorite toppings such as sour cream, salsa, or sliced jalapeños.

Tips:

- **For extra flavor:** Add chopped green chilies or diced tomatoes to the cheese filling.
- **For a spicier sauce:** Increase the amount of chili powder or add a pinch of cayenne pepper.
- **Make ahead:** Assemble the enchiladas and freeze them before baking. Thaw and bake as directed when ready to serve.

Cheese Enchiladas are a comforting and satisfying meal, perfect for any occasion. Enjoy!

Pork Tamales

Ingredients:

For the Pork Filling:

- **Pork Shoulder (or Pork Butt):** 3 lbs, trimmed and cut into large chunks
- **Olive Oil:** 2 tbsp
- **Onion:** 1, chopped
- **Garlic:** 4 cloves, minced
- **Chili Powder:** 2 tbsp
- **Ground Cumin:** 1 tsp
- **Paprika:** 1 tsp
- **Dried Oregano:** 1 tsp
- **Salt:** 1 1/2 tsp
- **Black Pepper:** 1 tsp
- **Tomato Paste:** 2 tbsp
- **Beef Broth:** 1 cup
- **Bay Leaves:** 2
- **Fresh Cilantro:** Chopped, for garnish (optional)

For the Masa Dough:

- **Corn Masa (Masa Harina):** 4 cups
- **Baking Powder:** 1 tbsp
- **Salt:** 1 tsp
- **Lard or Vegetable Shortening:** 1 cup (softened)
- **Chicken Broth:** 2 cups (or more if needed)

For Assembling:

- **Corn Husks:** 20-30, soaked in warm water for at least 1 hour (or until pliable)
- **Parchment Paper:** Cut into strips, optional (to prevent sticking)

Instructions:

1. **Prepare the Pork Filling:**
    - **Cook the Pork:** Heat olive oil in a large pot or Dutch oven over medium-high heat. Add pork chunks and sear on all sides until browned, about 5-7 minutes. Remove the pork and set aside.
    - **Sauté Aromatics:** In the same pot, add chopped onion and cook until softened, about 3-4 minutes. Stir in minced garlic and cook for another minute.

- **Add Spices and Tomato Paste:** Stir in chili powder, ground cumin, paprika, dried oregano, salt, and black pepper. Cook for 1-2 minutes. Add tomato paste and cook for another minute.
- **Simmer:** Return the pork to the pot. Add beef broth and bay leaves. Bring to a simmer, cover, and cook on low heat for 2-3 hours, or until the pork is tender and shreds easily.
- **Shred the Pork:** Remove pork from the pot, shred with two forks, and return it to the pot. Stir to combine with the sauce. Adjust seasoning if needed. Let cool.

2. **Prepare the Masa Dough:**
   - **Mix Dry Ingredients:** In a large bowl, combine corn masa, baking powder, and salt.
   - **Add Lard/Shortening:** Using your hands or a pastry cutter, work the softened lard or vegetable shortening into the masa mixture until it resembles coarse crumbs.
   - **Add Broth:** Gradually add chicken broth, mixing until the masa dough is smooth and pliable. The dough should be moist but not sticky.

3. **Assemble the Tamales:**
   - **Prepare Corn Husks:** Drain and pat the soaked corn husks dry. Tear a few husks into strips to use for tying the tamales.
   - **Spread Masa:** Place a husk on a flat surface. Spread about 2 tablespoons of masa dough in the center of the husk, leaving about 1 inch on each side.
   - **Add Filling:** Place a spoonful of the pork filling in the center of the masa.
   - **Fold and Roll:** Fold the sides of the husk over the masa and filling. Fold up the bottom of the husk to secure the tamale. Tie with a strip of husk if needed.

4. **Steam the Tamales:**
   - **Prepare Steamer:** Arrange a large steamer with a layer of soaked corn husks or a steaming rack to keep tamales from touching the water.
   - **Steam Tamales:** Stand tamales upright in the steamer. Cover with additional soaked husks or a clean kitchen towel to retain moisture. Steam over boiling water for 1 to 1 1/2 hours, or until the masa is fully cooked and pulls away from the husks easily. Check the water level occasionally and add more as needed.

5. **Serve:**
   - **Let Cool:** Allow tamales to cool slightly before serving.
   - **Garnish:** Garnish with chopped fresh cilantro if desired. Serve with salsa, sour cream, or your favorite toppings.

Tips:

- **For extra flavor:** Add a few tablespoons of salsa or green chilies to the pork filling.
- **For a smoother masa:** Be sure the lard or shortening is well incorporated and that the dough is not too dry. Add more chicken broth if necessary.
- **Make ahead:** Tamales can be made in advance and frozen. Steam directly from frozen, adding extra time as needed.

Enjoy your homemade Pork Tamales, a delicious and hearty dish that's perfect for special occasions or any time you're craving authentic Mexican comfort food!

Chimichangas

Ingredients:

For the Beef Filling:

- **Ground Beef:** 1 lb
- **Olive Oil:** 1 tbsp
- **Onion:** 1/2 cup, finely chopped
- **Garlic:** 2 cloves, minced
- **Ground Cumin:** 1 tsp
- **Chili Powder:** 1 tbsp
- **Paprika:** 1/2 tsp
- **Ground Coriander:** 1/2 tsp
- **Salt:** 1 tsp
- **Black Pepper:** 1/2 tsp
- **Refried Beans:** 1 cup
- **Shredded Cheese:** 1 cup (cheddar, Monterey Jack, or Mexican blend)
- **Chopped Fresh Cilantro:** For garnish (optional)

For Assembling:

- **Flour Tortillas:** 6-8 (8-inch size)
- **Vegetable Oil:** For frying

For Toppings (Optional):

- **Sour Cream:** For serving
- **Salsa or Pico de Gallo:** For serving
- **Guacamole:** For serving
- **Shredded Lettuce:** For serving
- **Diced Tomatoes:** For serving

Instructions:

1. **Prepare the Beef Filling:**
   - **Cook the Beef:** Heat olive oil in a large skillet over medium heat. Add the ground beef and cook until browned, breaking it up with a spoon as it cooks, about 6-8 minutes. Drain any excess fat.
   - **Add Aromatics and Spices:** Add chopped onion and cook until softened, about 3-4 minutes. Stir in minced garlic and cook for another minute. Add ground cumin, chili powder, paprika, ground coriander, salt, and black pepper. Mix well.

- **Combine Ingredients:** Stir in refried beans and shredded cheese. Cook for another 2-3 minutes, or until the cheese is melted and everything is well combined. Remove from heat.

2. **Assemble the Chimichangas:**
   - **Prepare Tortillas:** Heat tortillas in a dry skillet or microwave until warm and pliable.
   - **Fill Tortillas:** Place a generous amount of the beef mixture in the center of each tortilla. Fold in the sides and then roll up from the bottom to form a burrito. Secure the ends by tucking them in.

3. **Fry the Chimichangas:**
   - **Heat Oil:** In a large skillet or deep fryer, heat about 1-2 inches of vegetable oil to 350°F (175°C).
   - **Fry Chimichangas:** Carefully place the chimichangas in the hot oil, seam-side down. Fry in batches, if necessary, to avoid overcrowding. Cook for about 2-3 minutes per side, or until golden brown and crispy. Use tongs to turn them and ensure even cooking.
   - **Drain:** Remove the chimichangas from the oil and drain on paper towels.

4. **Serve:**
   - **Garnish:** Serve chimichangas hot, topped with your choice of sour cream, salsa, guacamole, shredded lettuce, and diced tomatoes. Garnish with chopped fresh cilantro if desired.

Tips:

- **For a healthier option:** Bake the chimichangas in a preheated oven at 400°F (200°C) for about 20-25 minutes, or until crispy and golden brown. Brush with a little oil before baking.
- **For extra flavor:** Add diced jalapeños, chopped green chilies, or a sprinkle of cayenne pepper to the beef filling.
- **Make-ahead:** Prepare and assemble the chimichangas ahead of time, and freeze them before frying. When ready to eat, fry directly from frozen, adding a couple of extra minutes to the cooking time.

Enjoy your homemade Beef Chimichangas, a crispy and satisfying dish that's sure to please!

Shrimp Ceviche

Ingredients:

- **Raw Shrimp:** 1 lb (peeled, deveined, and cut into small pieces)
- **Lime Juice:** 1 cup (freshly squeezed, about 8-10 limes)
- **Lemon Juice:** 1/4 cup (freshly squeezed)
- **Red Onion:** 1/2 cup, finely chopped
- **Tomato:** 1 cup, diced
- **Cucumber:** 1 cup, peeled, seeded, and diced
- **Jalapeño:** 1, seeded and finely chopped (adjust to taste)
- **Fresh Cilantro:** 1/4 cup, chopped
- **Avocado:** 1, diced
- **Salt:** 1/2 tsp (or to taste)
- **Black Pepper:** 1/4 tsp (or to taste)
- **Olive Oil:** 2 tbsp (optional, for a richer flavor)

For Serving:

- **Tortilla Chips:** For dipping
- **Lime Wedges:** For garnish

Instructions:

1. **Marinate the Shrimp:**
   - **Prepare Shrimp:** In a non-reactive bowl (such as glass or plastic), combine the shrimp with lime juice and lemon juice. Make sure the shrimp is fully submerged in the juice.
   - **Marinate:** Cover and refrigerate for about 2-3 hours, or until the shrimp turns pink and opaque. This indicates that the shrimp has "cooked" in the citrus juice.
2. **Combine Ingredients:**
   - **Drain Excess Juice:** After the shrimp is cooked, drain off excess citrus juice, leaving just a small amount to keep the ceviche moist.
   - **Mix Vegetables:** Add chopped red onion, diced tomato, diced cucumber, and chopped jalapeño to the shrimp. Stir to combine.
   - **Add Herbs and Seasoning:** Gently fold in chopped fresh cilantro, diced avocado, and olive oil (if using). Season with salt and black pepper to taste.
3. **Serve:**
   - **Chill:** For best flavor, let the ceviche chill in the refrigerator for an additional 30 minutes before serving.
   - **Garnish:** Serve chilled with tortilla chips and lime wedges on the side.

Tips:

- **For extra flavor:** Add a splash of hot sauce or a pinch of cayenne pepper if you like a bit of heat.
- **Freshness is key:** Use the freshest shrimp possible to ensure the best texture and flavor.
- **Serve immediately:** Ceviche is best enjoyed fresh, but it can be stored in the refrigerator for up to 2 days. Avoid freezing as it may affect the texture.

Enjoy your Shrimp Ceviche as a light and zesty appetizer or a refreshing meal on a warm day!

Chicken Tortilla Soup

Ingredients:

For the Soup:

- **Chicken Breasts or Thighs:** 1 lb, boneless and skinless
- **Olive Oil:** 2 tbsp
- **Onion:** 1 cup, chopped
- **Garlic:** 3 cloves, minced
- **Bell Pepper:** 1, chopped (red or green)
- **Carrot:** 1, chopped
- **Celery:** 1 stalk, chopped
- **Canned Diced Tomatoes:** 1 can (14.5 oz)
- **Chicken Broth:** 4 cups
- **Tortilla Chips or Strips:** 1 cup, crushed or sliced
- **Ground Cumin:** 1 tsp
- **Chili Powder:** 1 tbsp
- **Paprika:** 1/2 tsp
- **Dried Oregano:** 1/2 tsp
- **Salt:** 1 tsp (or to taste)
- **Black Pepper:** 1/2 tsp (or to taste)
- **Lime Juice:** 2 tbsp (freshly squeezed)
- **Corn Kernels:** 1 cup (fresh, frozen, or canned)
- **Fresh Cilantro:** 1/4 cup, chopped (for garnish)

For Toppings:

- **Shredded Cheese:** 1 cup (cheddar, Monterey Jack, or Mexican blend)
- **Diced Avocado:** 1
- **Sour Cream:** 1/2 cup
- **Chopped Fresh Cilantro:** For garnish
- **Lime Wedges:** For serving

Instructions:

1. **Cook the Chicken:**
    - **Poach Chicken:** In a large pot, add the chicken breasts or thighs and cover with water. Bring to a simmer over medium heat and cook until the chicken is cooked through and easily shreds, about 15-20 minutes. Remove chicken from the pot, shred it with two forks, and set aside. Discard cooking water or use it as part of the chicken broth if desired.
2. **Prepare the Soup Base:**

- **Sauté Vegetables:** In a large pot, heat olive oil over medium heat. Add chopped onion, garlic, bell pepper, carrot, and celery. Sauté until vegetables are softened, about 5-7 minutes.
- **Add Spices:** Stir in ground cumin, chili powder, paprika, and dried oregano. Cook for another minute to release the flavors.
- **Add Tomatoes and Broth:** Stir in diced tomatoes and chicken broth. Bring to a boil, then reduce heat and simmer for 10 minutes.

3. **Combine Ingredients:**
   - **Add Chicken and Corn:** Stir in the shredded chicken, corn kernels, and crushed tortilla chips or strips. Simmer for an additional 5-10 minutes, or until the corn is cooked through and the soup has thickened slightly.
   - **Season and Add Lime Juice:** Adjust seasoning with salt and black pepper to taste. Stir in lime juice.
4. **Serve:**
   - **Garnish:** Ladle soup into bowls and top with shredded cheese, diced avocado, and a dollop of sour cream. Garnish with additional chopped cilantro and serve with lime wedges on the side.

Tips:

- **For extra flavor:** Add a pinch of cayenne pepper or a splash of hot sauce if you like your soup spicy.
- **For a richer broth:** Use homemade chicken broth or add a bit of chicken bouillon for extra depth of flavor.
- **For a heartier soup:** Add black beans or pinto beans along with the chicken and corn.

Enjoy your Chicken Tortilla Soup, a warm and satisfying dish that's perfect for any day of the week!

Mexican Street Corn (Elote)

Ingredients:

- **Fresh Corn on the Cob:** 4 ears, husked and cleaned
- **Mayonnaise:** 1/2 cup
- **Sour Cream:** 1/4 cup (optional, for added creaminess)
- **Cotija Cheese:** 1/2 cup, crumbled (or use Parmesan if Cotija is unavailable)
- **Chili Powder:** 1 tsp
- **Paprika:** 1/2 tsp (smoked paprika adds extra flavor)
- **Garlic Powder:** 1/2 tsp
- **Lime Juice:** 2 tbsp (freshly squeezed)
- **Fresh Cilantro:** 2 tbsp, chopped (optional)
- **Salt:** To taste
- **Black Pepper:** To taste

Instructions:

1. **Prepare the Corn:**
    - **Husk the Corn:** Remove the husks and silks from the corn cobs. Rinse under cold water to remove any remaining silk.
2. **Grill the Corn:**
    - **Preheat Grill:** Preheat your grill to medium-high heat.
    - **Grill Corn:** Place the corn cobs on the grill. Cook, turning occasionally, until the corn is charred and cooked through, about 10-15 minutes. You should get a nice char on the kernels.
3. **Prepare the Topping:**
    - **Mix Sauce:** In a bowl, combine mayonnaise, sour cream (if using), crumbled Cotija cheese, chili powder, paprika, garlic powder, lime juice, and chopped cilantro. Stir until well combined.
4. **Assemble the Elote:**
    - **Coat the Corn:** Once the corn is grilled, remove it from the grill and brush or spread the creamy mixture over the hot corn, making sure to cover all sides.
    - **Season:** Sprinkle additional chili powder and a bit of salt and black pepper to taste. You can also sprinkle more Cotija cheese on top if desired.
5. **Serve:**
    - **Garnish and Enjoy:** Serve the elote hot with extra lime wedges on the side for squeezing over the top. Garnish with extra chopped cilantro if desired.

Tips:

- **For a smoky flavor:** Use smoked paprika instead of regular paprika.
- **To make it spicy:** Add a pinch of cayenne pepper or a few dashes of hot sauce to the creamy mixture.
- **For added texture:** Drizzle with a bit of extra melted butter before adding the topping.

Enjoy your Mexican Street Corn, a delicious and festive treat that's perfect for summer barbecues or any time you're craving something flavorful and fun!

Chile Rellenos

Ingredients:

For the Chile Rellenos:

- **Poblano Peppers:** 6 large (or 4 if they are very large)
- **Shredded Cheese:** 2 cups (cheddar, Monterey Jack, or a mix; Oaxaca cheese is traditional)
- **Ground Beef or Pork:** 1/2 lb (optional, for stuffed meat version)
- **Onion:** 1/2 cup, finely chopped (if using meat)
- **Garlic:** 2 cloves, minced (if using meat)
- **Tomato Sauce:** 1/2 cup (if using meat)
- **Cumin:** 1/2 tsp (if using meat)
- **Salt:** To taste
- **Black Pepper:** To taste

For the Batter:

- **Eggs:** 4 large, separated
- **All-Purpose Flour:** 1/2 cup
- **Cornstarch:** 2 tbsp
- **Baking Powder:** 1/2 tsp
- **Salt:** 1/4 tsp
- **Black Pepper:** 1/4 tsp
- **Milk:** 1/4 cup (or more if needed)

For Frying:

- **Vegetable Oil:** For frying

For Serving:

- **Salsa or Tomato Sauce:** For drizzling or dipping (optional)
- **Fresh Cilantro:** For garnish (optional)

Instructions:

1. **Prepare the Peppers:**
   - **Roast Peppers:** Preheat your oven to 400°F (200°C) or use a grill. Place the poblanos on a baking sheet or directly on the grill. Roast, turning occasionally, until the skins are blackened and blistered, about 10-15 minutes.
   - **Peel and Seed:** Transfer the roasted peppers to a bowl covered with plastic wrap and let them steam for about 10 minutes. This will make it easier to peel the skin

off. Peel the skins off the peppers, then carefully make a slit along one side and remove the seeds and membranes. Set aside.
2. **Prepare the Filling:**
   - **Cook Meat (optional):** If using ground meat, heat a skillet over medium heat with a little oil. Add the chopped onion and garlic, and cook until softened. Add the ground meat, cumin, salt, and black pepper. Cook until the meat is browned and fully cooked. Stir in tomato sauce and cook for another 2-3 minutes. Let cool slightly.
   - **Stuff Peppers:** Stuff each pepper with shredded cheese and/or the cooked meat mixture.
3. **Prepare the Batter:**
   - **Mix Dry Ingredients:** In a bowl, combine flour, cornstarch, baking powder, salt, and black pepper.
   - **Beat Eggs:** In another bowl, beat egg yolks until pale and thick. In a separate bowl, beat egg whites until stiff peaks form.
   - **Combine:** Gently fold the beaten egg whites into the egg yolks. Gradually fold in the dry ingredients. Add milk a little at a time until the batter reaches a thick but pourable consistency.
4. **Fry the Peppers:**
   - **Heat Oil:** In a large skillet or deep fryer, heat about 1-2 inches of vegetable oil to 350°F (175°C).
   - **Coat and Fry:** Dip each stuffed pepper into the batter, coating it completely. Carefully place the battered peppers in the hot oil and fry until golden brown and crispy, about 4-5 minutes, turning occasionally. Fry in batches if needed to avoid overcrowding the pan.
   - **Drain:** Remove the peppers with a slotted spoon and drain on paper towels.
5. **Serve:**
   - **Garnish:** Serve hot, garnished with fresh cilantro if desired. Drizzle with salsa or tomato sauce if you like.

Tips:

- **For a lighter batter:** Use a mixture of flour and cornstarch and ensure the egg whites are beaten to stiff peaks for a light, crispy coating.
- **For added flavor:** Season the cheese filling with herbs like oregano or a sprinkle of chili powder.
- **Make ahead:** Stuff and batter the peppers in advance, then freeze. Fry directly from frozen, adding a few extra minutes to the cooking time.

Enjoy your Chile Rellenos, a flavorful and satisfying dish that's sure to impress!

Beef Fajitas

Ingredients:

For the Marinade:

- **Beef Flank Steak or Skirt Steak:** 1 lb, thinly sliced
- **Olive Oil:** 1/4 cup
- **Lime Juice:** 2 tbsp (freshly squeezed)
- **Garlic:** 3 cloves, minced
- **Ground Cumin:** 1 tsp
- **Chili Powder:** 1 tsp
- **Paprika:** 1/2 tsp
- **Ground Coriander:** 1/2 tsp
- **Salt:** 1 tsp
- **Black Pepper:** 1/2 tsp
- **Cayenne Pepper:** 1/4 tsp (optional, for heat)

For the Fajitas:

- **Bell Peppers:** 2 (red and green), thinly sliced
- **Onion:** 1 large, thinly sliced
- **Olive Oil:** 2 tbsp (for sautéing)
- **Tortillas:** 8 small flour tortillas (or corn if preferred)
- **Fresh Cilantro:** For garnish

For Serving:

- **Sour Cream:** 1/2 cup
- **Shredded Cheese:** 1 cup (cheddar, Monterey Jack, or Mexican blend)
- **Salsa:** 1 cup
- **Guacamole:** 1/2 cup
- **Lime Wedges:** For serving
- **Shredded Lettuce:** For garnish (optional)
- **Diced Tomatoes:** For garnish (optional)

Instructions:

1. **Marinate the Beef:**
    - **Combine Marinade Ingredients:** In a bowl, whisk together olive oil, lime juice, minced garlic, ground cumin, chili powder, paprika, ground coriander, salt, black pepper, and cayenne pepper (if using).
    - **Marinate Beef:** Add the thinly sliced beef to the marinade and mix to coat evenly. Cover and refrigerate for at least 1 hour, or up to 4 hours for more flavor.

2. **Cook the Fajitas:**
    - **Preheat Skillet:** Heat 2 tablespoons of olive oil in a large skillet or cast-iron pan over medium-high heat.
    - **Sauté Vegetables:** Add the sliced bell peppers and onion to the skillet. Sauté for 5-7 minutes, or until the vegetables are tender and slightly charred. Remove from the skillet and set aside.
    - **Cook the Beef:** In the same skillet, add the marinated beef strips in a single layer. Cook for 3-4 minutes per side, or until the beef is cooked to your desired level of doneness and has a nice sear. Be careful not to overcrowd the pan; you may need to cook the beef in batches.
    - **Combine:** Return the sautéed bell peppers and onions to the skillet with the beef. Toss everything together and cook for an additional 1-2 minutes to combine flavors.
3. **Warm the Tortillas:**
    - **Heat Tortillas:** Warm the flour tortillas in a dry skillet over medium heat, or wrap them in foil and heat in a preheated oven at 350°F (175°C) for about 10 minutes.
4. **Serve:**
    - **Assemble Fajitas:** Serve the beef and vegetable mixture with warm tortillas and your choice of toppings. Garnish with fresh cilantro.
    - **Add Toppings:** Offer sour cream, shredded cheese, salsa, guacamole, lime wedges, shredded lettuce, and diced tomatoes for a customizable fajita experience.

Tips:

- **For the best flavor:** Let the beef marinate for as long as possible, up to 4 hours.
- **For a smoky taste:** Add a few drops of liquid smoke to the marinade.
- **For extra tenderness:** Use flank steak or skirt steak, which are ideal for fajitas due to their flavor and texture. Make sure to slice against the grain for tenderness.

Enjoy your Beef Fajitas, a delicious and satisfying dish perfect for a fun meal with family or friends!

Chicken Fajitas

Ingredients:

For the Marinade:

Chicken Breasts or Thighs: 1 lb, thinly sliced

Olive Oil: 1/4 cup

Lime Juice: 2 tbsp (freshly squeezed)

Garlic: 3 cloves, minced

Ground Cumin: 1 tsp

Chili Powder: 1 tsp

Paprika: 1/2 tsp

Ground Coriander: 1/2 tsp

Salt: 1 tsp

Black Pepper: 1/2 tsp

Cayenne Pepper: 1/4 tsp (optional, for heat)

For the Fajitas:

Bell Peppers: 2 (red and green), thinly sliced

Onion: 1 large, thinly sliced

Olive Oil: 2 tbsp (for sautéing)

Tortillas: 8 small flour tortillas (or corn if preferred)

Fresh Cilantro: For garnish

For Serving:

Sour Cream: 1/2 cup

Shredded Cheese: 1 cup (cheddar, Monterey Jack, or Mexican blend)

Salsa: 1 cup

Guacamole: 1/2 cup

Lime Wedges: For serving

Shredded Lettuce: For garnish (optional)

Diced Tomatoes: For garnish (optional)

Instructions:

Marinate the Chicken:

Prepare Marinade: In a bowl, whisk together olive oil, lime juice, minced garlic, ground cumin, chili powder, paprika, ground coriander, salt, black pepper, and cayenne pepper (if using).

Marinate Chicken: Add the thinly sliced chicken to the marinade and mix well to coat. Cover and refrigerate for at least 30 minutes, or up to 4 hours for more flavor.

Cook the Fajitas:

Preheat Skillet: Heat 2 tablespoons of olive oil in a large skillet or cast-iron pan over medium-high heat.

Sauté Vegetables: Add the sliced bell peppers and onions to the skillet. Sauté for about 5-7 minutes, or until the vegetables are tender and slightly charred. Remove from the skillet and set aside.

Cook the Chicken: In the same skillet, add the marinated chicken strips in a single layer. Cook for 5-7 minutes, stirring occasionally, until the chicken is cooked through and has a nice sear. Be careful not to overcrowd the pan; you may need to cook the chicken in batches.

Combine: Return the sautéed bell peppers and onions to the skillet with the chicken. Toss everything together and cook for an additional 1-2 minutes to combine the flavors.

Warm the Tortillas:

Heat Tortillas: Warm the flour tortillas in a dry skillet over medium heat, or wrap them in foil and heat in a preheated oven at 350°F (175°C) for about 10 minutes.

Serve:

Assemble Fajitas: Serve the chicken and vegetable mixture with warm tortillas and your choice of toppings. Garnish with fresh cilantro.

Add Toppings: Offer sour cream, shredded cheese, salsa, guacamole, lime wedges, shredded lettuce, and diced tomatoes for a customizable fajita experience.

Tips:

For the best flavor: Allow the chicken to marinate for as long as possible. If you're short on time, even 30 minutes will make a difference.

For a smoky taste: Add a few drops of liquid smoke to the marinade.

For extra tenderness: Use chicken thighs instead of breasts for a juicier result, or slice the chicken against the grain for tenderness.

Enjoy your Chicken Fajitas, a delightful and versatile dish that's perfect for a fun family meal or a casual dinner with friends!

Huevos Rancheros

Ingredients:

For the Ranchero Sauce:

- **Tomatoes:** 4 medium, peeled and chopped (or use 1 can (14.5 oz) of diced tomatoes)
- **Onion:** 1 small, chopped
- **Garlic:** 2 cloves, minced
- **Green Chile:** 1-2 (fresh or canned, seeded and chopped, or 1 can (4 oz) of diced green chilies)
- **Ground Cumin:** 1/2 tsp
- **Chili Powder:** 1 tsp
- **Paprika:** 1/2 tsp
- **Salt:** 1/2 tsp (or to taste)
- **Black Pepper:** 1/4 tsp
- **Olive Oil:** 1 tbsp
- **Fresh Cilantro:** 2 tbsp, chopped (optional)

For the Huevos Rancheros:

- **Corn Tortillas:** 4
- **Eggs:** 4
- **Vegetable Oil:** For frying
- **Refried Beans:** 1 cup (optional, for spreading on tortillas)
- **Shredded Cheese:** 1/2 cup (optional, for garnish)
- **Avocado:** 1, sliced (for garnish)
- **Fresh Cilantro:** For garnish
- **Lime Wedges:** For serving

Instructions:

1. **Make the Ranchero Sauce:**
    - **Sauté Vegetables:** Heat olive oil in a skillet over medium heat. Add chopped onion and cook until translucent, about 5 minutes.
    - **Add Garlic and Green Chile:** Stir in minced garlic and chopped green chile. Cook for another 1-2 minutes.
    - **Add Tomatoes and Spices:** Add chopped tomatoes (or canned tomatoes) along with ground cumin, chili powder, paprika, salt, and black pepper. Simmer the sauce over low heat for 10-15 minutes, until thickened. Stir occasionally.
    - **Adjust Flavor:** Taste and adjust seasoning as needed. Stir in chopped cilantro if desired.
2. **Prepare the Tortillas:**

- **Warm Tortillas:** Heat the corn tortillas on a dry skillet over medium heat until warmed and slightly crispy, or wrap in foil and heat in the oven. Keep warm.

3. **Cook the Eggs:**
   - **Fry Eggs:** In a separate skillet, heat a little vegetable oil over medium heat. Crack the eggs into the skillet and cook until the whites are set but the yolks are still runny, or cook to your desired level of doneness. You can also cook them sunny-side up or over-easy.

4. **Assemble the Huevos Rancheros:**
   - **Spread Beans (Optional):** If using, spread a layer of refried beans on each tortilla.
   - **Top with Sauce:** Place the tortillas on plates and spoon a generous amount of the ranchero sauce over each.
   - **Add Eggs:** Top each tortilla with a fried egg.
   - **Garnish:** Sprinkle with shredded cheese if using, and garnish with sliced avocado, fresh cilantro, and additional lime wedges.

5. **Serve:**
   - **Enjoy:** Serve immediately with lime wedges on the side for extra flavor.

Tips:

- **For extra flavor:** Add a pinch of cayenne pepper to the ranchero sauce if you like it spicier.
- **For a richer sauce:** Blend the ranchero sauce for a smoother texture if desired.
- **Make ahead:** The ranchero sauce can be made ahead of time and stored in the refrigerator for up to 4 days.

Huevos Rancheros is a versatile dish that's perfect for breakfast or brunch. Enjoy the combination of savory, spicy, and fresh flavors!

Pork Pozole

Ingredients:

For the Pozole:

- **Pork Shoulder:** 2 lbs, cut into chunks
- **Hominy:** 2 cans (15.5 oz each) or about 4 cups of frozen or fresh hominy (drained and rinsed if canned)
- **Pork Broth or Chicken Broth:** 6 cups
- **Onion:** 1 large, chopped
- **Garlic:** 4 cloves, minced
- **Dried Pasilla Chiles:** 2, seeds removed (or use 1-2 tbsp of pasilla chile powder if you can't find dried chiles)
- **Dried Ancho Chiles:** 2, seeds removed (or use 1-2 tbsp of ancho chile powder)
- **Ground Cumin:** 1 tsp
- **Oregano:** 1 tsp (Mexican oregano is traditional, but regular oregano works too)
- **Bay Leaves:** 2
- **Salt:** 1-2 tsp (to taste)
- **Black Pepper:** 1/2 tsp (or to taste)
- **Vegetable Oil:** 2 tbsp

For Garnishing:

- **Shredded Cabbage:** 2 cups
- **Radishes:** 1 cup, thinly sliced
- **Diced Avocado:** 1
- **Lime Wedges:** For serving
- **Chopped Cilantro:** 1/4 cup
- **Sour Cream:** 1/2 cup
- **Tortilla Chips or Crispy Tortilla Strips:** For serving
- **Sliced Jalapeños:** (optional, for added heat)

Instructions:

1. **Prepare the Chiles:**
   - **Toast Chiles:** Heat a dry skillet over medium heat. Toast the dried pasilla and ancho chiles for about 1-2 minutes, turning frequently, until fragrant but not burnt. Remove from heat.
   - **Soak Chiles:** Place the toasted chiles in a bowl and cover with hot water. Let them soak for about 15 minutes until softened.
   - **Blend Chiles:** Drain the chiles and blend them with a little bit of water until smooth. You should have about 1/2 cup of chile paste.
2. **Cook the Pork:**

- **Brown Pork:** Heat vegetable oil in a large pot over medium-high heat. Add pork chunks and cook until browned on all sides. Remove the pork from the pot and set aside.

3. **Prepare the Pozole:**
   - **Sauté Aromatics:** In the same pot, add chopped onion and cook until translucent, about 5 minutes. Add minced garlic and cook for another minute.
   - **Add Chile Paste and Spices:** Stir in the chile paste, ground cumin, oregano, bay leaves, salt, and black pepper. Cook for another 2 minutes.
   - **Add Pork and Broth:** Return the browned pork to the pot. Pour in the pork or chicken broth. Bring to a boil, then reduce the heat to low and simmer for 1.5-2 hours, or until the pork is tender and can be easily shredded with a fork.
   - **Add Hominy:** Stir in the drained hominy and continue to cook for another 30 minutes, or until the hominy is heated through and has absorbed some of the flavors.
4. **Serve:**
   - **Garnish and Enjoy:** Ladle the pozole into bowls. Garnish with shredded cabbage, sliced radishes, diced avocado, chopped cilantro, and a dollop of sour cream. Serve with lime wedges, tortilla chips, or crispy tortilla strips on the side. Add sliced jalapeños if you like extra heat.

Tips:

- **For deeper flavor:** Let the pozole simmer for a few hours if you have the time; the flavors will develop even more.
- **For a spicier pozole:** Add more chili paste or a splash of hot sauce to taste.
- **For a smoother broth:** Blend some of the pozole with an immersion blender before adding the hominy, then return the blended mixture to the pot.

Enjoy your Pork Pozole, a comforting and hearty dish that's perfect for family gatherings or a satisfying meal any time!

Sopes

Ingredients:

For the Sopes:

- **Corn Masa:** 2 cups (store-bought masa harina or fresh masa; if using masa harina, mix with 1 1/4 cups warm water to form a dough)
- **All-Purpose Flour:** 1/4 cup (for dusting)
- **Salt:** 1/2 tsp
- **Vegetable Oil:** For frying

For the Toppings:

- **Refried Beans:** 1 cup (black or pinto beans)
- **Cooked Meat:** 1 cup (shredded beef, chicken, or pork, optional)
- **Shredded Lettuce:** 1 cup
- **Chopped Tomatoes:** 1 cup
- **Sour Cream:** 1/2 cup
- **Shredded Cheese:** 1/2 cup (queso fresco, cotija, or cheddar)
- **Sliced Jalapeños:** (optional, for heat)
- **Chopped Cilantro:** For garnish
- **Salsa:** For drizzling

Instructions:

1. **Prepare the Masa:**
    - **Mix Masa:** If using masa harina, mix 2 cups of masa harina with 1 1/4 cups warm water and 1/2 tsp salt to form a smooth dough. If using fresh masa, just add the salt.
    - **Divide Dough:** Divide the dough into 8-10 equal balls, about 1.5 inches in diameter.
2. **Shape the Sopes:**
    - **Flatten Dough:** Lightly flour a surface and a rolling pin. Flatten each dough ball into a 4-5 inch round, about 1/4 inch thick.
    - **Form the Edges:** Use your fingers or a small, round object to gently pinch the edges of each round to create a raised border about 1/2 inch high. This helps hold the toppings in place.
3. **Cook the Sopes:**
    - **Heat Oil:** Heat a small amount of vegetable oil in a skillet over medium heat.
    - **Cook Sopes:** Cook each sope in the hot skillet for about 2 minutes per side, until golden brown. You may need to press down gently with a spatula to ensure even cooking. Remove from the skillet and drain on paper towels.
4. **Top the Sopes:**

- **Spread Beans:** Spread a layer of refried beans over each sope.
            - **Add Meat (if using):** Top with cooked meat if desired.
            - **Add Fresh Toppings:** Add shredded lettuce, chopped tomatoes, shredded cheese, and any additional toppings you like.
            - **Finish:** Drizzle with sour cream, salsa, and sprinkle with chopped cilantro.
    5. **Serve:**
        - **Enjoy:** Serve the sopes warm with your choice of sides and additional salsa.

Tips:

- **For a crispy texture:** Make sure to fry the sopes until they are golden brown and slightly crispy on the edges.
- **To keep warm:** If making in batches, keep the cooked sopes warm in a low oven (200°F or 90°C) until ready to serve.
- **Customize Toppings:** Sopes are highly versatile; feel free to add other toppings like avocado slices, pickled onions, or hot sauce.

Sopes are a delicious and customizable dish that's perfect for sharing or enjoying on your own. Enjoy the combination of crispy, savory, and fresh flavors!

Mexican Rice

Ingredients:

- **Vegetable Oil:** 2 tbsp
- **Long-Grain White Rice:** 1 cup
- **Onion:** 1 small, finely chopped
- **Garlic:** 2 cloves, minced
- **Tomato Sauce:** 1 cup (or 1-2 ripe tomatoes blended into a puree)
- **Chicken Broth:** 2 cups (or vegetable broth for a vegetarian version)
- **Carrots:** 1/2 cup, diced (optional)
- **Frozen Peas:** 1/2 cup (optional)
- **Ground Cumin:** 1/2 tsp
- **Chili Powder:** 1/2 tsp
- **Paprika:** 1/2 tsp
- **Salt:** 1 tsp (or to taste)
- **Black Pepper:** 1/4 tsp
- **Fresh Cilantro:** For garnish (optional)
- **Lime Wedges:** For serving (optional)

Instructions:

1. **Toast the Rice:**
   - **Heat Oil:** In a large skillet or saucepan, heat the vegetable oil over medium heat.
   - **Cook Rice:** Add the rice and cook, stirring frequently, until the rice turns a light golden brown, about 5-7 minutes. Be careful not to burn the rice.
2. **Sauté Aromatics:**
   - **Add Onion:** Add the chopped onion to the skillet with the rice and cook until the onion is translucent, about 3 minutes.
   - **Add Garlic:** Stir in the minced garlic and cook for another minute until fragrant.
3. **Add Tomato and Spices:**
   - **Stir in Tomato Sauce:** Add the tomato sauce (or tomato puree) to the rice and mix well.
   - **Add Spices:** Stir in the ground cumin, chili powder, paprika, salt, and black pepper.
4. **Add Broth and Vegetables:**
   - **Pour in Broth:** Add the chicken or vegetable broth to the skillet and bring to a boil.
   - **Add Carrots and Peas (Optional):** Stir in the diced carrots and frozen peas if using.
   - **Simmer:** Reduce the heat to low, cover the skillet, and simmer for 18-20 minutes, or until the rice is tender and the liquid is absorbed.
5. **Fluff and Serve:**

- - **Fluff Rice:** Once the rice is cooked, remove from heat and let it sit, covered, for about 5 minutes. Then, fluff the rice with a fork to separate the grains.
  - **Garnish:** Garnish with fresh cilantro if desired and serve with lime wedges on the side.

Tips:

- **For extra flavor:** Sauté the rice with a bit of minced bell pepper or jalapeño along with the onion and garlic.
- **For a richer color:** Use a bit of saffron or turmeric in addition to the spices.
- **Make ahead:** Mexican Rice can be made ahead of time and reheated. It also freezes well.

Enjoy your Mexican Rice as a flavorful and versatile side dish that complements a wide range of Mexican and Tex-Mex meals!

Refried Beans

Ingredients:

- **Pinto Beans or Black Beans:** 2 cups dried beans (or 4 cups canned beans)
- **Water:** For soaking and cooking (if using dried beans)
- **Vegetable Oil or Lard:** 2-3 tbsp (lard is traditional, but vegetable oil is a common substitute)
- **Onion:** 1 small, finely chopped
- **Garlic:** 2 cloves, minced
- **Ground Cumin:** 1/2 tsp
- **Chili Powder:** 1/2 tsp
- **Salt:** 1 tsp (or to taste)
- **Black Pepper:** 1/4 tsp
- **Chicken Broth or Vegetable Broth:** 1/2 cup (optional, for added flavor)
- **Fresh Cilantro:** For garnish (optional)

Instructions:

1. **Prepare the Beans:**
    - **Soak Dried Beans:** If using dried beans, rinse them and place them in a large bowl. Cover with water and soak overnight. Drain and rinse the beans before cooking.
    - **Cook Beans:** In a large pot, cover the soaked beans with fresh water. Bring to a boil, then reduce the heat and simmer for 1.5 to 2 hours, or until the beans are tender. You can also use a pressure cooker or Instant Pot to speed up the process. Once cooked, drain the beans, reserving some of the cooking liquid.
2. **Cook the Beans:**
    - **Heat Fat:** In a large skillet or saucepan, heat the vegetable oil or lard over medium heat.
    - **Sauté Aromatics:** Add the chopped onion and cook until translucent, about 5 minutes. Add the minced garlic and cook for another minute until fragrant.
    - **Add Beans and Spices:** Stir in the cooked beans, ground cumin, chili powder, salt, and black pepper. If the beans are too thick, add some of the reserved cooking liquid or broth to reach your desired consistency.
3. **Mash the Beans:**
    - **Mash Beans:** Use a potato masher or the back of a spoon to mash the beans to your desired consistency. For smoother beans, you can use an immersion blender or food processor.
    - **Fry Beans:** Continue to cook the beans, stirring frequently, until they reach a creamy consistency and are heated through. If needed, add more liquid to keep them from getting too dry.
4. **Serve:**

- **Garnish and Enjoy:** Garnish with fresh cilantro if desired. Serve warm as a side dish or as part of various Mexican dishes.

Tips:

- **For extra flavor:** Add a pinch of smoked paprika or a dash of hot sauce to the beans.
- **For a richer taste:** Use lard or bacon fat instead of vegetable oil for a more authentic flavor.
- **Make ahead:** Refried beans can be made ahead of time and stored in the refrigerator for up to a week or frozen for up to 3 months.

Refried Beans are perfect as a side dish, in tacos, burritos, or nachos, and they add a wonderful, comforting element to any meal. Enjoy!

Tostadas

Ingredients:

For the Tostada Shells:

- **Corn Tortillas:** 8-10 (store-bought or homemade)
- **Vegetable Oil:** For frying (or you can bake them for a healthier version)

For the Toppings:

- **Refried Beans:** 1 cup (black or pinto beans)
- **Shredded Lettuce:** 2 cups
- **Chopped Tomatoes:** 1 cup
- **Shredded Cheese:** 1 cup (queso fresco, cheddar, or Mexican blend)
- **Cooked Meat:** 1 cup (shredded chicken, beef, or pork, optional)
- **Avocado:** 1, sliced
- **Sour Cream:** 1/2 cup
- **Salsa:** 1/2 cup
- **Chopped Cilantro:** For garnish
- **Lime Wedges:** For serving
- **Sliced Jalapeños:** (optional, for heat)

Instructions:

1. **Prepare the Tostada Shells:**
    - **Fry Tortillas:**
        - **Heat Oil:** In a large skillet, heat about 1/2 inch of vegetable oil over medium heat.
        - **Fry Tortillas:** Fry the corn tortillas one at a time until they are crispy and golden brown, about 1-2 minutes per side. Use tongs to flip them and drain on paper towels.
    - **Bake Tortillas (for a healthier option):**
        - **Preheat Oven:** Preheat your oven to 400°F (200°C).
        - **Prepare Tortillas:** Brush both sides of the tortillas with a small amount of oil and place them in a single layer on a baking sheet.
        - **Bake:** Bake for about 5-7 minutes, flipping halfway through, until they are crispy and golden brown.
2. **Assemble the Tostadas:**
    - **Spread Beans:** Spread a layer of refried beans over each crispy tortilla.
    - **Add Meat (optional):** Top with cooked meat if using.
    - **Add Fresh Toppings:** Layer with shredded lettuce, chopped tomatoes, and shredded cheese.

- **Garnish:** Add sliced avocado, sour cream, salsa, and chopped cilantro. Top with sliced jalapeños if you like extra heat.
3. **Serve:**
    - **Enjoy:** Serve the tostadas immediately while the shells are still crispy. Provide lime wedges on the side for added flavor.

Tips:

- **Customize Toppings:** Feel free to add other toppings such as pickled onions, radishes, or black olives.
- **Make Ahead:** You can prepare the tostada shells ahead of time and store them in an airtight container. Assemble the tostadas just before serving to keep the shells crispy.
- **For Extra Flavor:** Add a sprinkle of chili powder or a dash of hot sauce to the toppings for an extra kick.

Tostadas are perfect for a casual meal or party, allowing everyone to customize their own with their favorite ingredients. Enjoy your crispy, flavorful tostadas!

Baja Fish Tacos

Ingredients:

For the Fish:

- **White Fish Fillets:** 1 lb (such as cod, tilapia, or haddock)
- **Flour:** 1 cup
- **Cornstarch:** 1/4 cup
- **Baking Powder:** 1 tsp
- **Salt:** 1 tsp
- **Ground Black Pepper:** 1/2 tsp
- **Paprika:** 1/2 tsp
- **Garlic Powder:** 1/2 tsp
- **Cold Sparkling Water or Beer:** 1 cup
- **Vegetable Oil:** For frying (about 2 cups)

For the Baja Sauce:

- **Mayonnaise:** 1/2 cup
- **Sour Cream:** 1/4 cup
- **Lime Juice:** 2 tbsp (freshly squeezed)
- **Chipotle Powder:** 1/2 tsp
- **Garlic Powder:** 1/2 tsp
- **Salt:** 1/4 tsp (or to taste)

For the Toppings:

- **Shredded Cabbage:** 2 cups
- **Chopped Cilantro:** 1/4 cup
- **Sliced Radishes:** 1/2 cup
- **Diced Tomatoes:** 1 cup
- **Sliced Jalapeños:** (optional, for heat)
- **Lime Wedges:** For serving

For the Tacos:

- **Corn or Flour Tortillas:** 8-10 (preferably small size)

Instructions:

1. **Prepare the Fish:**
    - **Cut Fish:** Cut the fish fillets into strips or bite-sized pieces.

- **Season Flour:** In a shallow dish, mix together the flour, cornstarch, baking powder, salt, black pepper, paprika, and garlic powder.
- **Coat Fish:** Dredge the fish pieces in the seasoned flour mixture, shaking off excess. Dip the coated fish pieces into the cold sparkling water or beer to coat in the batter, then coat again in the flour mixture for a double-crisp effect.

2. **Fry the Fish:**
   - **Heat Oil:** In a large skillet or deep fryer, heat the vegetable oil over medium-high heat to 350°F (175°C).
   - **Fry Fish:** Fry the fish in batches, being careful not to overcrowd the pan. Cook until golden brown and crispy, about 3-4 minutes per side. Remove with a slotted spoon and drain on paper towels.
3. **Make the Baja Sauce:**
   - **Mix Ingredients:** In a small bowl, combine the mayonnaise, sour cream, lime juice, chipotle powder, garlic powder, and salt. Stir until well mixed and smooth.
4. **Prepare the Toppings:**
   - **Prepare Vegetables:** Shred the cabbage, chop the cilantro, slice the radishes, and dice the tomatoes. Set aside.
5. **Warm the Tortillas:**
   - **Heat Tortillas:** Warm the tortillas on a dry skillet over medium heat or wrap them in foil and heat them in the oven until soft and pliable.
6. **Assemble the Tacos:**
   - **Spread Sauce:** Spread a spoonful of Baja sauce on each tortilla.
   - **Add Fish:** Top with a few pieces of fried fish.
   - **Add Toppings:** Add shredded cabbage, chopped cilantro, sliced radishes, diced tomatoes, and sliced jalapeños if using.
   - **Finish:** Drizzle with additional Baja sauce and serve with lime wedges on the side.
7. **Serve:**
   - **Enjoy:** Serve the tacos immediately while the fish is still warm and crispy.

Tips:

- **For a lighter version:** You can bake the fish instead of frying it. Coat the fish with the batter and bake at 400°F (200°C) for about 15-20 minutes or until crispy and cooked through.
- **Customize:** Add other toppings like avocado slices or pickled onions for additional flavor and texture.
- **Make Ahead:** Prepare the Baja sauce and toppings ahead of time to streamline the process when you're ready to assemble the tacos.

Enjoy your Baja Fish Tacos with their crispy fish, creamy sauce, and fresh toppings for a delightful and satisfying meal!

Chicken Tostadas

Ingredients:

For the Chicken:

- **Boneless, Skinless Chicken Breasts or Thighs:** 1 lb
- **Olive Oil:** 1 tbsp
- **Garlic:** 2 cloves, minced
- **Ground Cumin:** 1/2 tsp
- **Chili Powder:** 1/2 tsp
- **Paprika:** 1/2 tsp
- **Ground Coriander:** 1/2 tsp
- **Salt:** 1 tsp
- **Black Pepper:** 1/4 tsp
- **Chicken Broth:** 1/2 cup (or water)
- **Lime Juice:** 1 tbsp (optional, for extra flavor)

For the Tostada Shells:

- **Corn Tortillas:** 8-10 (store-bought or homemade)
- **Vegetable Oil:** For frying (or you can bake them for a healthier option)

For the Toppings:

- **Refried Beans:** 1 cup (black or pinto beans)
- **Shredded Lettuce:** 2 cups
- **Chopped Tomatoes:** 1 cup
- **Shredded Cheese:** 1 cup (queso fresco, cheddar, or Mexican blend)
- **Sliced Avocado:** 1-2
- **Sour Cream:** 1/2 cup
- **Salsa:** 1/2 cup
- **Chopped Cilantro:** For garnish
- **Lime Wedges:** For serving
- **Sliced Jalapeños:** (optional, for heat)

Instructions:

1. **Prepare the Chicken:**
   - **Season Chicken:** In a bowl, mix together the garlic, ground cumin, chili powder, paprika, ground coriander, salt, and black pepper. Rub this mixture onto the chicken breasts or thighs.
   - **Cook Chicken:** Heat olive oil in a skillet over medium heat. Add the seasoned chicken and cook for about 6-8 minutes per side, or until fully cooked and the

internal temperature reaches 165°F (74°C). If using thighs, cook until tender and easily shred with a fork.
   - **Shred Chicken:** Once cooked, remove the chicken from the skillet and let it rest for a few minutes before shredding it with two forks. If desired, stir in lime juice for extra flavor.
2. **Prepare the Tostada Shells:**
   - **Fry Tortillas:** Heat vegetable oil in a large skillet over medium heat. Fry the corn tortillas one at a time until they are crispy and golden brown, about 1-2 minutes per side. Drain on paper towels.
   - **Bake Tortillas (for a healthier option):** Preheat oven to 400°F (200°C). Brush both sides of the tortillas with a small amount of oil and place them in a single layer on a baking sheet. Bake for about 5-7 minutes, flipping halfway through, until crispy and golden brown.
3. **Assemble the Tostadas:**
   - **Spread Beans:** Spread a layer of refried beans over each crispy tortilla.
   - **Add Chicken:** Top with shredded chicken.
   - **Add Fresh Toppings:** Layer with shredded lettuce, chopped tomatoes, shredded cheese, and sliced avocado.
   - **Finish:** Drizzle with sour cream, salsa, and garnish with chopped cilantro. Add sliced jalapeños if you like extra heat.
4. **Serve:**
   - **Enjoy:** Serve the tostadas immediately while the shells are still crispy. Provide lime wedges on the side for added flavor.

Tips:

- **Customize:** Feel free to add other toppings like pickled onions, radishes, or a sprinkle of hot sauce for extra flavor.
- **Make Ahead:** You can prepare the chicken and toppings ahead of time. Assemble the tostadas just before serving to keep the shells crispy.
- **For Extra Flavor:** Marinate the chicken in the seasoning mixture for a few hours or overnight for a more intense flavor.

Chicken Tostadas are a great way to enjoy a variety of fresh and flavorful ingredients on a crispy base. Enjoy your homemade tostadas!

Beef Taquitos

Ingredients:

For the Beef Filling:

- **Ground Beef:** 1 lb
- **Onion:** 1 small, finely chopped
- **Garlic:** 2 cloves, minced
- **Ground Cumin:** 1/2 tsp
- **Chili Powder:** 1/2 tsp
- **Paprika:** 1/2 tsp
- **Oregano:** 1/2 tsp
- **Salt:** 1 tsp
- **Black Pepper:** 1/4 tsp
- **Tomato Paste:** 2 tbsp
- **Beef Broth:** 1/4 cup (or water)
- **Vegetable Oil:** For frying

For the Taquitos:

- **Corn Tortillas:** 12-15 (store-bought or homemade)
- **Shredded Cheese:** 1 cup (optional, for added flavor)

For Serving:

- **Sour Cream:** For dipping
- **Salsa:** For dipping
- **Chopped Cilantro:** For garnish
- **Lime Wedges:** For serving
- **Sliced Jalapeños:** (optional, for heat)

Instructions:

1. **Prepare the Beef Filling:**
    - **Cook Beef:** In a large skillet over medium heat, add the ground beef and cook until browned, breaking it apart with a spoon as it cooks.
    - **Add Onion and Garlic:** Add the chopped onion and minced garlic to the skillet and cook until the onion is translucent, about 5 minutes.
    - **Add Spices and Tomato Paste:** Stir in the ground cumin, chili powder, paprika, oregano, salt, and black pepper. Add the tomato paste and cook for another 2 minutes, stirring frequently.

- **Add Broth:** Pour in the beef broth and cook for an additional 5 minutes, or until the mixture has thickened and most of the liquid has evaporated. Remove from heat and let the filling cool slightly.
2. **Prepare the Tortillas:**
    - **Heat Tortillas:** To make the tortillas pliable, heat them in a dry skillet over medium heat for about 30 seconds per side, or wrap them in a damp paper towel and microwave for 30 seconds.
3. **Assemble the Taquitos:**
    - **Fill Tortillas:** Place a small amount of the beef filling in the center of each tortilla. Optionally, sprinkle with shredded cheese.
    - **Roll Tortillas:** Roll the tortillas tightly around the filling, securing with a toothpick if needed.
4. **Fry the Taquitos:**
    - **Heat Oil:** In a large skillet, heat about 1/2 inch of vegetable oil over medium heat to 350°F (175°C).
    - **Fry Taquitos:** Fry the taquitos in batches, turning occasionally, until they are golden brown and crispy, about 3-4 minutes. Use tongs to transfer them to a plate lined with paper towels to drain excess oil.
5. **Serve:**
    - **Enjoy:** Serve the taquitos warm with sour cream, salsa, and lime wedges. Garnish with chopped cilantro and sliced jalapeños if desired.

Tips:

- **For a healthier version:** Bake the taquitos instead of frying. Brush them lightly with oil and bake at 400°F (200°C) for 15-20 minutes, turning halfway through, until crispy and golden brown.
- **Customize:** Feel free to add other ingredients to the filling, such as diced bell peppers or black beans.
- **Make Ahead:** You can prepare the beef filling and tortillas ahead of time. Assemble and fry the taquitos just before serving.

Enjoy your homemade Beef Taquitos with their crispy exterior and flavorful beef filling!

Chili Con Carne

Ingredients:

For the Chili:

- **Ground Beef:** 1 lb (85% lean or higher)
- **Onion:** 1 large, chopped
- **Garlic:** 3 cloves, minced
- **Bell Pepper:** 1 large, chopped (any color)
- **Carrots:** 2 medium, diced (optional, for added sweetness)
- **Tomato Paste:** 2 tbsp
- **Diced Tomatoes:** 1 can (14.5 oz)
- **Kidney Beans:** 1 can (15 oz), drained and rinsed
- **Black Beans:** 1 can (15 oz), drained and rinsed
- **Beef Broth:** 1 cup (or water)
- **Chili Powder:** 2 tbsp
- **Ground Cumin:** 1 tsp
- **Paprika:** 1 tsp
- **Oregano:** 1 tsp
- **Ground Coriander:** 1/2 tsp
- **Salt:** 1 tsp (or to taste)
- **Black Pepper:** 1/2 tsp (or to taste)
- **Cayenne Pepper:** 1/4 tsp (optional, for heat)
- **Bay Leaf:** 1
- **Olive Oil:** 2 tbsp

For Garnishing:

- **Shredded Cheese:** Cheddar or Mexican blend
- **Sour Cream**
- **Chopped Cilantro**
- **Sliced Jalapeños:** (optional, for extra heat)
- **Chopped Green Onions:** (optional)

Instructions:

1. **Cook the Beef:**
   - **Heat Oil:** In a large pot or Dutch oven, heat the olive oil over medium-high heat.
   - **Brown Beef:** Add the ground beef and cook, breaking it apart with a spoon, until it is browned and no longer pink. Drain excess fat if necessary.
2. **Add Vegetables:**
   - **Sauté Aromatics:** Add the chopped onion, garlic, bell pepper, and carrots (if using) to the pot. Cook until the vegetables are softened, about 5-7 minutes.

3. **Add Tomato and Spices:**
   - **Stir in Tomato Paste:** Add the tomato paste and cook for about 2 minutes, stirring constantly.
   - **Add Tomatoes and Beans:** Stir in the diced tomatoes, kidney beans, black beans, and beef broth.
   - **Add Spices:** Stir in the chili powder, ground cumin, paprika, oregano, ground coriander, salt, black pepper, cayenne pepper (if using), and bay leaf.
4. **Simmer the Chili:**
   - **Bring to a Boil:** Bring the chili to a boil, then reduce the heat to low.
   - **Simmer:** Cover and let the chili simmer for 30-45 minutes, stirring occasionally, until the flavors are well combined and the chili has thickened to your liking.
5. **Adjust Seasoning:**
   - **Taste and Adjust:** Taste the chili and adjust seasoning as needed, adding more salt, pepper, or chili powder if desired.
6. **Serve:**
   - **Garnish:** Serve the chili hot, garnished with shredded cheese, sour cream, chopped cilantro, sliced jalapeños, and green onions if desired.

Tips:

- **For Extra Flavor:** You can add a splash of Worcestershire sauce or a bit of dark chocolate for depth of flavor.
- **For a Smoky Kick:** Add a teaspoon of smoked paprika or chipotle powder.
- **Make Ahead:** Chili Con Carne can be made ahead of time and often tastes even better the next day. It can be refrigerated for up to 3 days or frozen for up to 3 months.

Enjoy your hearty and flavorful Chili Con Carne!

Mexican Stuffed Peppers

Ingredients:

For the Stuffed Peppers:

- **Bell Peppers:** 4 large (any color, tops cut off and seeds removed)
- **Ground Beef or Ground Turkey:** 1 lb
- **Onion:** 1 small, finely chopped
- **Garlic:** 2 cloves, minced
- **Cooked Rice:** 1 cup (white or brown)
- **Black Beans:** 1 can (15 oz), drained and rinsed
- **Corn:** 1 cup (fresh, frozen, or canned)
- **Diced Tomatoes:** 1 can (14.5 oz)
- **Chili Powder:** 1 tsp
- **Ground Cumin:** 1/2 tsp
- **Paprika:** 1/2 tsp
- **Oregano:** 1/2 tsp
- **Salt:** 1 tsp
- **Black Pepper:** 1/4 tsp
- **Shredded Cheese:** 1 cup (cheddar, Monterey Jack, or Mexican blend)
- **Fresh Cilantro:** For garnish (optional)
- **Lime Wedges:** For serving (optional)

Instructions:

1. **Prepare the Peppers:**
    - **Preheat Oven:** Preheat your oven to 375°F (190°C).
    - **Prepare Peppers:** Cut the tops off the bell peppers and remove the seeds and membranes. If needed, trim the bottoms slightly so they stand upright. Place the peppers in a baking dish, cut side up.
2. **Cook the Filling:**
    - **Brown Meat:** In a large skillet, heat a bit of oil over medium heat. Add the ground beef or turkey and cook until browned, breaking it apart with a spoon. Drain any excess fat.
    - **Add Vegetables:** Add the chopped onion and minced garlic to the skillet. Cook until the onion is translucent, about 5 minutes.
    - **Mix Ingredients:** Stir in the cooked rice, black beans, corn, diced tomatoes, chili powder, ground cumin, paprika, oregano, salt, and black pepper. Cook for another 5 minutes, allowing the flavors to meld together.
3. **Stuff the Peppers:**
    - **Fill Peppers:** Spoon the meat mixture into each bell pepper, packing it in firmly.
    - **Top with Cheese:** Sprinkle shredded cheese on top of each stuffed pepper.

4. **Bake the Peppers:**
   - **Cover and Bake:** Cover the baking dish with aluminum foil and bake in the preheated oven for 30 minutes.
   - **Uncover and Bake:** Remove the foil and bake for an additional 10-15 minutes, or until the peppers are tender and the cheese is melted and bubbly.
5. **Serve:**
   - **Garnish and Enjoy:** Garnish with fresh cilantro if desired and serve with lime wedges on the side for a burst of fresh flavor.

Tips:

- **For a Spicier Kick:** Add some diced jalapeños or a dash of hot sauce to the filling.
- **For Extra Flavor:** Mix in some taco seasoning or a splash of lime juice into the meat mixture.
- **Make Ahead:** You can prepare the stuffed peppers ahead of time and refrigerate them for up to 2 days. Bake them just before serving.

These Mexican Stuffed Peppers are a flavorful and filling meal that combines the best of Mexican ingredients in a fun and nutritious package. Enjoy!

Burrito Bowls

Ingredients:

For the Base:

- **Cooked Rice:** 2 cups (white, brown, or cilantro-lime rice)
- **Cooked Beans:** 1 can (15 oz) of black beans or pinto beans, drained and rinsed
- **Corn:** 1 cup (fresh, frozen, or canned)
- **Chopped Romaine Lettuce:** 2 cups

For the Protein:

- **Cooked Chicken:** 1 lb (shredded or diced) or
- **Ground Beef:** 1 lb (cooked and seasoned) or
- **Cooked Tofu:** 1 lb (cubed, for a vegetarian option)

For the Seasoned Meat (if using chicken or beef):

- **Olive Oil:** 1 tbsp
- **Chili Powder:** 1 tbsp
- **Ground Cumin:** 1 tsp
- **Paprika:** 1/2 tsp
- **Garlic Powder:** 1/2 tsp
- **Onion Powder:** 1/2 tsp
- **Salt:** 1 tsp
- **Black Pepper:** 1/2 tsp

For the Toppings:

- **Diced Tomatoes:** 1 cup
- **Sliced Avocado:** 1-2 (or guacamole)
- **Shredded Cheese:** 1 cup (cheddar, Monterey Jack, or Mexican blend)
- **Sour Cream:** 1/2 cup
- **Salsa:** 1/2 cup
- **Chopped Cilantro:** For garnish
- **Lime Wedges:** For serving

Instructions:

1. **Prepare the Protein:**
    - **For Chicken:**
        - **Season and Cook:** Season the chicken with chili powder, ground cumin, paprika, garlic powder, onion powder, salt, and black pepper. Cook in a

skillet with olive oil over medium heat until fully cooked. Shred or dice as desired.
- **For Ground Beef:**
  - **Season and Cook:** Cook the ground beef in a skillet until browned. Drain excess fat, then stir in chili powder, ground cumin, paprika, garlic powder, onion powder, salt, and black pepper. Cook until well combined and heated through.
- **For Tofu:**
  - **Season and Cook:** Toss cubed tofu with a bit of soy sauce and your choice of seasoning. Sauté in a pan with a little oil until golden and crispy.
2. **Prepare the Base:**
   - **Cook Rice:** Prepare rice according to package instructions. For cilantro-lime rice, mix cooked rice with fresh lime juice and chopped cilantro.
   - **Prepare Beans and Corn:** Heat beans and corn in a saucepan until warmed through. Season with a pinch of salt and pepper if desired.
3. **Assemble the Bowls:**
   - **Layer Ingredients:** In each bowl, start with a base of rice. Add a portion of beans and corn.
   - **Add Protein:** Top with your choice of protein (chicken, beef, or tofu).
   - **Add Fresh Toppings:** Layer with chopped lettuce, diced tomatoes, and sliced avocado. Sprinkle with shredded cheese.
4. **Add Condiments:**
   - **Finish:** Add a dollop of sour cream and a spoonful of salsa on top. Garnish with chopped cilantro.
5. **Serve:**
   - **Enjoy:** Serve the burrito bowls with lime wedges on the side for a fresh squeeze of lime juice.

Tips:

- **Customize Your Bowl:** Feel free to add other ingredients such as pickled onions, jalapeños, or sautéed peppers and onions.
- **Make It Spicy:** Add hot sauce or chopped fresh chilies if you like extra heat.
- **Meal Prep:** These bowls are perfect for meal prep. Prepare ingredients in advance and assemble bowls as needed.

Burrito Bowls are a versatile and satisfying meal option that allows you to enjoy all your favorite burrito ingredients in a customizable bowl. Enjoy your tasty and hearty Burrito Bowls!

Green Chile Chicken Enchiladas

Ingredients:

For the Chicken Filling:

- **Cooked Chicken:** 2 cups, shredded (use rotisserie chicken or poach your own)
- **Olive Oil:** 1 tbsp
- **Onion:** 1 small, finely chopped
- **Garlic:** 2 cloves, minced
- **Green Chiles:** 1 can (4 oz) diced, or use fresh roasted green chiles if available
- **Cumin:** 1 tsp
- **Chili Powder:** 1/2 tsp
- **Salt:** 1/2 tsp
- **Black Pepper:** 1/4 tsp
- **Shredded Cheese:** 1 cup (Monterey Jack, cheddar, or Mexican blend)
- **Cilantro:** 1/4 cup, chopped (optional)

For the Green Chile Sauce:

- **Olive Oil:** 2 tbsp
- **Flour:** 2 tbsp
- **Chicken Broth:** 1 cup
- **Green Chiles:** 1 can (4 oz), diced
- **Sour Cream:** 1/2 cup
- **Salt:** 1/2 tsp
- **Black Pepper:** 1/4 tsp

For Assembly:

- **Corn Tortillas:** 10-12
- **Shredded Cheese:** 1-2 cups (for topping)
- **Chopped Cilantro:** For garnish (optional)
- **Sour Cream:** For serving (optional)
- **Sliced Jalapeños:** For garnish (optional)

Instructions:

1. **Prepare the Chicken Filling:**
   - **Cook Aromatics:** In a large skillet, heat olive oil over medium heat. Add the chopped onion and garlic, and cook until the onion is translucent, about 5 minutes.
   - **Add Chicken and Spices:** Stir in the shredded chicken, diced green chiles, cumin, chili powder, salt, and black pepper. Cook for another 2-3 minutes,

allowing the flavors to meld. Remove from heat and stir in the shredded cheese and chopped cilantro if using. Set aside.

2. **Prepare the Green Chile Sauce:**
   - **Make Roux:** In a saucepan, heat olive oil over medium heat. Add the flour and cook, stirring constantly, for about 1-2 minutes until it forms a light roux (a thickening base for the sauce).
   - **Add Broth and Chiles:** Gradually whisk in the chicken broth, and then add the diced green chiles. Continue to cook, stirring frequently, until the sauce thickens, about 5-7 minutes.
   - **Finish Sauce:** Stir in the sour cream, salt, and black pepper. Cook for an additional 2 minutes. Remove from heat.
3. **Assemble the Enchiladas:**
   - **Prepare Tortillas:** Heat the corn tortillas in a dry skillet or on a griddle over medium heat until they are pliable. Alternatively, you can wrap them in a damp paper towel and microwave for about 30 seconds.
   - **Fill Tortillas:** Spoon a portion of the chicken mixture onto each tortilla, then roll them up tightly.
   - **Place in Baking Dish:** Arrange the rolled tortillas seam-side down in a greased baking dish.
   - **Top with Sauce:** Pour the green chile sauce over the rolled tortillas, spreading it evenly.
4. **Bake the Enchiladas:**
   - **Add Cheese:** Sprinkle the top with additional shredded cheese.
   - **Bake:** Bake in a preheated oven at 375°F (190°C) for 20-25 minutes, or until the cheese is melted and bubbly, and the sauce is bubbling.
5. **Serve:**
   - **Garnish and Enjoy:** Garnish with chopped cilantro, if desired. Serve with sour cream, sliced jalapeños, and additional garnishes as preferred.

Tips:

- **Make-Ahead:** You can prepare the enchiladas in advance and store them in the refrigerator for up to 2 days before baking. Just cover them tightly with plastic wrap or aluminum foil.
- **Freezing:** Enchiladas can be frozen before baking. Assemble them, cover with plastic wrap and foil, and freeze for up to 3 months. Bake from frozen, adding 10-15 minutes to the cooking time.
- **Spice Level:** Adjust the amount of green chiles to control the heat level of your enchiladas.

Enjoy these Green Chile Chicken Enchiladas as a comforting and flavorful meal!

Mexican Chilaquiles

Ingredients:

For the Chips:

- **Corn Tortillas:** 8-10, cut into triangles or strips
- **Vegetable Oil:** For frying (about 1-2 cups)
- **Salt:** To taste

For the Sauce:

Green Sauce:

- **Tomatillos:** 1 lb, husked and rinsed
- **Green Chilies:** 2 (such as jalapeños or serranos), stemmed and seeded (adjust to your heat preference)
- **Garlic:** 2 cloves
- **Onion:** 1 small, chopped
- **Cilantro:** 1/4 cup, chopped
- **Lime Juice:** 2 tbsp
- **Salt:** 1/2 tsp
- **Chicken or Vegetable Broth:** 1/2 cup

Red Sauce:

- **Dried Chiles:** 4-5 (such as ancho or guajillo), stemmed and seeded
- **Tomatoes:** 4 large, chopped (or 1 can of diced tomatoes)
- **Garlic:** 2 cloves
- **Onion:** 1 small, chopped
- **Cumin:** 1/2 tsp
- **Oregano:** 1/2 tsp
- **Salt:** 1/2 tsp
- **Chicken or Vegetable Broth:** 1/2 cup

For Topping:

- **Fried Eggs:** 4 (one per serving)
- **Crumbled Cotija Cheese:** 1/2 cup (or feta cheese)
- **Chopped Cilantro:** For garnish
- **Thinly Sliced Radishes:** For garnish
- **Sour Cream:** For garnish
- **Avocado:** Sliced, for garnish
- **Lime Wedges:** For serving

Instructions:

1. **Prepare the Chips:**
   - **Heat Oil:** In a large skillet or deep fryer, heat the vegetable oil over medium-high heat.
   - **Fry Tortillas:** Fry the tortilla triangles in batches until they are crispy and golden brown, about 2-3 minutes per batch. Remove with a slotted spoon and drain on paper towels. Sprinkle with salt immediately while still hot.
2. **Make the Sauce:**

   For Green Sauce:
   - **Cook Tomatillos and Chilies:** In a saucepan, cook the tomatillos, green chilies, and garlic over medium heat until softened, about 10 minutes. You can also roast them for extra flavor.
   - **Blend:** Transfer the cooked ingredients to a blender. Add the chopped onion, cilantro, lime juice, and salt. Blend until smooth. Return the sauce to the pan and add chicken or vegetable broth to achieve your desired consistency. Simmer for 5 minutes.
3. **For Red Sauce:**
   - **Toast Chiles:** In a dry skillet, toast the dried chiles over medium heat until fragrant, about 1-2 minutes. Be careful not to burn them.
   - **Blend Sauce:** In a blender, combine the toasted chiles, chopped tomatoes, garlic, onion, cumin, oregano, and salt. Blend until smooth. Add the chicken or vegetable broth and blend again. Pour the mixture into a saucepan and simmer for 10 minutes, stirring occasionally.
4. **Combine Chips and Sauce:**
   - **Simmer Chips:** Pour the sauce over the fried tortilla chips in the skillet. Stir to coat the chips evenly with the sauce. Cook over medium heat until the chips are softened but still slightly crispy, about 3-5 minutes. Be careful not to overcook or the chips will become too soggy.
5. **Serve:**
   - **Top and Garnish:** Divide the chilaquiles among serving plates. Top each with a fried egg, crumbled cotija cheese, chopped cilantro, sliced radishes, sour cream, and avocado slices.
   - **Serve with Lime Wedges:** Serve with lime wedges on the side for extra zest.

Tips:

- **Sauce Choice:** Both red and green sauces are delicious. Choose based on your taste preference or make both and let everyone choose their favorite.
- **Make It Spicy:** Adjust the amount of chilies in the sauce to control the heat level. For extra heat, add a splash of hot sauce.
- **Make Ahead:** You can prepare the sauce in advance and store it in the refrigerator for up to a week. Reheat before mixing with the chips.

Enjoy your Chilaquiles as a satisfying breakfast or brunch dish, and savor the vibrant flavors of Mexican cuisine!

Beef and Bean Burritos

Ingredients:

For the Beef Filling:

- **Ground Beef:** 1 lb (85% lean or higher)
- **Onion:** 1 small, chopped
- **Garlic:** 2 cloves, minced
- **Chili Powder:** 1 tbsp
- **Ground Cumin:** 1 tsp
- **Paprika:** 1/2 tsp
- **Oregano:** 1/2 tsp
- **Salt:** 1/2 tsp
- **Black Pepper:** 1/4 tsp
- **Tomato Sauce:** 1/2 cup
- **Beef Broth:** 1/4 cup (or water)
- **Black Beans:** 1 can (15 oz), drained and rinsed
- **Refried Beans:** 1 cup (store-bought or homemade)
- **Shredded Cheese:** 1 cup (cheddar, Monterey Jack, or Mexican blend)

For Assembly:

- **Flour Tortillas:** 8 large (burrito-sized)
- **Sour Cream:** 1/2 cup
- **Salsa:** 1/2 cup
- **Chopped Lettuce:** 1 cup
- **Diced Tomatoes:** 1 cup
- **Sliced Jalapeños:** For garnish (optional)
- **Chopped Cilantro:** For garnish (optional)

Instructions:

1. **Prepare the Beef Filling:**
   - **Cook Beef:** In a large skillet, heat a bit of oil over medium heat. Add the chopped onion and cook until softened, about 5 minutes.
   - **Add Garlic:** Stir in the minced garlic and cook for another minute.
   - **Brown Beef:** Add the ground beef to the skillet. Cook, breaking it apart with a spoon, until it is browned and fully cooked. Drain any excess fat.
   - **Season Meat:** Stir in the chili powder, ground cumin, paprika, oregano, salt, and black pepper. Mix well.
   - **Add Tomato Sauce and Broth:** Pour in the tomato sauce and beef broth. Stir to combine and let it simmer for about 5 minutes until the sauce thickens slightly.

- **Add Beans:** Stir in the black beans and refried beans. Cook until the beans are heated through and everything is well combined.
2. **Assemble the Burritos:**
    - **Warm Tortillas:** Heat the flour tortillas in a dry skillet or in the microwave until they are warm and pliable.
    - **Fill Tortillas:** Place a tortilla on a flat surface. Spoon a portion of the beef and bean mixture down the center of the tortilla. Top with a sprinkle of shredded cheese.
    - **Roll Burritos:** Fold the sides of the tortilla over the filling, then roll it up from the bottom to enclose the filling completely. Repeat with the remaining tortillas and filling.
3. **Serve:**
    - **Garnish:** Serve the burritos with a dollop of sour cream, salsa, chopped lettuce, diced tomatoes, and any additional garnishes you like, such as sliced jalapeños or chopped cilantro.

Tips:

- **Customization:** Feel free to add other ingredients to the filling, such as sautéed peppers, onions, or corn.
- **Make Ahead:** You can assemble the burritos in advance and refrigerate them for up to 2 days before serving. Reheat them in a skillet or oven to warm through.
- **Freezing:** Burritos can be frozen for up to 3 months. Wrap them tightly in foil or plastic wrap and freeze. Reheat from frozen in the oven at 375°F (190°C) for about 30-40 minutes, or until heated through.

Beef and Bean Burritos are a satisfying and versatile meal that you can easily adapt to suit your tastes. Enjoy your delicious and filling burritos!

Chicken and Cheese Nachos

Ingredients:

For the Chicken:

- **Cooked Chicken:** 2 cups, shredded or diced (rotisserie chicken works great)
- **Olive Oil:** 1 tbsp
- **Onion:** 1 small, chopped
- **Garlic:** 2 cloves, minced
- **Chili Powder:** 1 tsp
- **Ground Cumin:** 1/2 tsp
- **Paprika:** 1/2 tsp
- **Oregano:** 1/2 tsp
- **Salt:** 1/2 tsp
- **Black Pepper:** 1/4 tsp
- **Salsa:** 1/2 cup (or use diced tomatoes for a milder option)
- **Lime Juice:** 1 tbsp (optional)

For the Nachos:

- **Tortilla Chips:** 1 large bag (or homemade chips)
- **Shredded Cheese:** 2 cups (cheddar, Monterey Jack, or Mexican blend)
- **Black Beans:** 1 can (15 oz), drained and rinsed (optional)
- **Corn:** 1 cup (fresh, frozen, or canned)
- **Sliced Jalapeños:** 1/4 cup (adjust to taste)
- **Chopped Cilantro:** For garnish

For Toppings:

- **Sour Cream:** 1/2 cup
- **Guacamole:** 1/2 cup
- **Salsa:** 1/2 cup
- **Diced Tomatoes:** 1 cup
- **Chopped Green Onions:** 1/4 cup
- **Sliced Black Olives:** 1/4 cup (optional)

Instructions:

1. **Prepare the Chicken:**
    - **Cook Aromatics:** In a skillet, heat olive oil over medium heat. Add the chopped onion and cook until softened, about 5 minutes. Add minced garlic and cook for another minute.

- **Add Chicken and Spices:** Stir in the shredded or diced chicken, chili powder, ground cumin, paprika, oregano, salt, and black pepper. Cook for a few minutes until the chicken is well-coated with spices and heated through.
- **Add Salsa:** Stir in the salsa and cook for another 2-3 minutes. If desired, add lime juice for a touch of brightness. Remove from heat.

2. **Assemble the Nachos:**
    - **Preheat Oven:** Preheat your oven to 400°F (200°C).
    - **Layer Chips:** On a large baking sheet or oven-safe dish, spread out a layer of tortilla chips.
    - **Add Chicken:** Evenly distribute the cooked chicken over the chips.
    - **Add Beans and Corn:** Sprinkle black beans (if using) and corn over the chicken.
    - **Top with Cheese:** Generously sprinkle shredded cheese over the entire layer.
3. **Bake the Nachos:**
    - **Bake:** Place the baking sheet or dish in the preheated oven and bake for 10-15 minutes, or until the cheese is melted and bubbly and the chips are crispy.
    - **Broil (Optional):** For extra crispiness, you can switch to broil for an additional 2-3 minutes, but watch carefully to prevent burning.
4. **Add Toppings:**
    - **Garnish:** Remove from the oven and immediately sprinkle with sliced jalapeños and chopped cilantro.
    - **Serve with Sides:** Serve with a variety of toppings on the side, such as sour cream, guacamole, salsa, diced tomatoes, chopped green onions, and sliced black olives.

Tips:

- **Customize:** Feel free to add other toppings like sliced bell peppers, chopped red onions, or pickled jalapeños for extra flavor.
- **Make Ahead:** You can prepare the chicken mixture ahead of time and store it in the refrigerator until you're ready to assemble and bake the nachos.
- **For Extra Crunch:** If you like your nachos extra crispy, you can bake the tortilla chips separately for a few minutes before adding the toppings.

Enjoy your Chicken and Cheese Nachos as a tasty snack, appetizer, or meal!

Mexican Meatballs (Albondigas)

Ingredients:

For the Meatballs:

- **Ground Beef:** 1 lb
- **Ground Pork:** 1/2 lb (optional; you can use all beef if preferred)
- **Egg:** 1, lightly beaten
- **Breadcrumbs:** 1/2 cup (or use crushed tortilla chips for extra flavor)
- **Garlic:** 2 cloves, minced
- **Onion:** 1 small, finely chopped
- **Cilantro:** 1/4 cup, chopped
- **Cumin:** 1/2 tsp
- **Paprika:** 1/2 tsp
- **Chili Powder:** 1 tsp
- **Salt:** 1/2 tsp
- **Black Pepper:** 1/4 tsp
- **Zucchini:** 1 small, grated (optional, for added moisture and nutrition)

For the Soup Base:

- **Olive Oil:** 2 tbsp
- **Onion:** 1 small, chopped
- **Garlic:** 2 cloves, minced
- **Carrots:** 2, peeled and sliced
- **Celery:** 2 stalks, sliced
- **Tomato Sauce:** 1 can (15 oz) or 2 cups of homemade tomato sauce
- **Chicken Broth:** 4 cups
- **Canned Diced Tomatoes:** 1 can (14.5 oz)
- **Bay Leaves:** 2
- **Cumin:** 1/2 tsp
- **Oregano:** 1/2 tsp
- **Salt:** To taste
- **Black Pepper:** To taste
- **Chopped Cilantro:** For garnish
- **Lime Wedges:** For serving

Instructions:

1. **Prepare the Meatballs:**
    - **Mix Ingredients:** In a large bowl, combine the ground beef, ground pork (if using), beaten egg, breadcrumbs, minced garlic, chopped onion, cilantro, cumin,

paprika, chili powder, salt, and black pepper. Mix until well combined, but do not overmix.
   - **Form Meatballs:** Shape the mixture into 1-inch meatballs and set aside on a plate.
2. **Prepare the Soup Base:**
   - **Cook Aromatics:** In a large pot or Dutch oven, heat olive oil over medium heat. Add the chopped onion and cook until softened, about 5 minutes. Add minced garlic and cook for another minute.
   - **Add Vegetables:** Stir in the sliced carrots and celery. Cook for 5 minutes until they start to soften.
   - **Add Tomato Sauce and Broth:** Pour in the tomato sauce, chicken broth, and canned diced tomatoes. Stir to combine.
   - **Season:** Add bay leaves, cumin, oregano, salt, and black pepper. Bring the mixture to a simmer.
3. **Cook the Meatballs:**
   - **Add Meatballs:** Gently drop the meatballs into the simmering soup. Do not stir too vigorously to avoid breaking the meatballs.
   - **Simmer:** Let the meatballs cook in the simmering broth for about 20-25 minutes, or until they are cooked through and reach an internal temperature of 160°F (71°C). The soup will thicken slightly as it cooks.
4. **Serve:**
   - **Garnish and Enjoy:** Remove the bay leaves. Ladle the meatballs and soup into bowls. Garnish with chopped cilantro and serve with lime wedges on the side for a fresh squeeze of lime juice.

Tips:

- **Customization:** Feel free to add other vegetables to the soup, such as potatoes, corn, or bell peppers, according to your preference.
- **Spice Level:** Adjust the amount of chili powder and cumin to control the spice level of the dish.
- **Make-Ahead:** Albondigas can be made in advance and stored in the refrigerator for up to 3 days. The flavors tend to deepen and improve over time.

Enjoy your Mexican Meatballs (Albondigas) with a side of warm tortillas or crusty bread for a complete and satisfying meal!

Spicy Pork Carnitas

Ingredients:

For the Pork:

- **Pork Shoulder (Pork Butt):** 3-4 lbs, cut into large chunks
- **Olive Oil:** 2 tbsp
- **Onion:** 1 large, chopped
- **Garlic:** 4 cloves, minced
- **Chili Powder:** 2 tbsp
- **Cumin:** 1 tbsp
- **Paprika:** 1 tbsp
- **Dried Oregano:** 1 tbsp
- **Cayenne Pepper:** 1/2 tsp (adjust for heat level)
- **Salt:** 1 tsp
- **Black Pepper:** 1/2 tsp
- **Orange Juice:** 1 cup (or use a mix of orange juice and lime juice)
- **Lime Juice:** 2 tbsp (optional, for extra tanginess)
- **Bay Leaves:** 2
- **Chicken Broth:** 1 cup

For Crisping (Optional but recommended):

- **Vegetable Oil:** 2 tbsp (for frying the carnitas after slow cooking)

Instructions:

1. **Prepare the Pork:**
   - **Season Pork:** In a large bowl, combine the chili powder, cumin, paprika, dried oregano, cayenne pepper, salt, and black pepper. Rub this spice mixture all over the pork chunks, making sure each piece is well-coated.
2. **Cook the Pork:**
   - **Sear Pork:** Heat olive oil in a large Dutch oven or heavy-bottomed pot over medium-high heat. Add the pork chunks in batches, searing on all sides until browned. Remove the pork and set aside.
   - **Cook Aromatics:** In the same pot, add the chopped onion and cook until softened, about 5 minutes. Add the minced garlic and cook for an additional minute.
   - **Combine Ingredients:** Return the seared pork to the pot. Pour in the orange juice, lime juice (if using), and chicken broth. Add bay leaves and stir to combine.
   - **Simmer:** Bring the mixture to a simmer, then cover and reduce the heat to low. Cook for 2.5 to 3 hours, or until the pork is tender and easily shredable.
3. **Shred the Pork:**

- **Remove Pork:** Once the pork is tender, remove it from the pot and place it on a large cutting board. Discard the bay leaves.
- **Shred:** Using two forks, shred the pork into bite-sized pieces.
4. **Crisp the Carnitas (Optional but recommended):**
    - **Preheat Oven or Skillet:** Preheat your oven to 400°F (200°C) or heat a large skillet over medium-high heat.
    - **Crisp Pork:** Spread the shredded pork on a baking sheet or in a skillet. Drizzle with vegetable oil and bake for 15-20 minutes, or until the edges of the pork become crispy and caramelized. If using a skillet, cook for 5-10 minutes, stirring occasionally, until the edges are crispy.
5. **Serve:**
    - **Enjoy:** Serve the spicy pork carnitas with your favorite toppings and sides, such as warm tortillas, chopped cilantro, diced onions, lime wedges, salsa, and avocado.

Tips:

- **Adjust Spice Level:** Customize the spiciness by adjusting the amount of cayenne pepper or adding extra chili powder.
- **Make-Ahead:** Carnitas can be made ahead of time and stored in the refrigerator for up to 4 days or frozen for up to 3 months. Reheat in a skillet to regain some crispiness.
- **Alternative Cooking Methods:** For a more hands-off approach, you can also cook the carnitas in a slow cooker or instant pot. For the slow cooker, cook on low for 6-8 hours. For the instant pot, use the pressure cook function for about 45 minutes.

Enjoy your spicy, flavorful Pork Carnitas in tacos, burritos, or even as a main dish with some fresh sides!

Black Bean Soup

Ingredients:

- **Olive Oil:** 2 tbsp
- **Onion:** 1 large, chopped
- **Garlic:** 3 cloves, minced
- **Carrots:** 2, peeled and chopped
- **Celery:** 2 stalks, chopped
- **Bell Pepper:** 1, chopped (any color)
- **Cumin:** 1 tsp
- **Paprika:** 1 tsp
- **Chili Powder:** 1 tsp
- **Oregano:** 1/2 tsp
- **Black Beans:** 3 cans (15 oz each), drained and rinsed (or 4 cups cooked black beans)
- **Tomatoes:** 1 can (14.5 oz) diced tomatoes with green chilies (or plain diced tomatoes)
- **Vegetable Broth:** 4 cups (or chicken broth)
- **Bay Leaves:** 2
- **Salt:** To taste
- **Black Pepper:** To taste
- **Lime Juice:** 2 tbsp (optional, for added flavor)
- **Fresh Cilantro:** For garnish

Optional Toppings:

- **Sour Cream**
- **Shredded Cheese:** Cheddar or Monterey Jack
- **Diced Avocado**
- **Chopped Green Onions**
- **Tortilla Chips:** Crumbled or whole

Instructions:

1. **Sauté Vegetables:**
    - **Heat Oil:** In a large pot, heat the olive oil over medium heat.
    - **Cook Aromatics:** Add the chopped onion and cook until translucent, about 5 minutes. Add the minced garlic and cook for another minute.
    - **Add Vegetables:** Stir in the chopped carrots, celery, and bell pepper. Cook until the vegetables start to soften, about 5-7 minutes.
2. **Add Spices:**
    - **Season:** Stir in the cumin, paprika, chili powder, and oregano. Cook for 1-2 minutes until fragrant.
3. **Combine Ingredients:**
    - **Add Beans and Tomatoes:** Add the black beans, diced tomatoes (with their juices), and vegetable broth to the pot. Stir to combine.
    - **Add Bay Leaves:** Drop in the bay leaves.
4. **Simmer:**

- **Cook Soup:** Bring the mixture to a boil, then reduce the heat and let it simmer for 20-30 minutes. The vegetables should be tender, and the flavors will meld together.
5. **Blend (Optional):**
    - **Puree Soup:** For a smoother texture, use an immersion blender to partially blend the soup directly in the pot, or carefully transfer half of the soup to a blender, blend until smooth, and return it to the pot. Alternatively, you can leave the soup chunky.
6. **Season and Finish:**
    - **Adjust Seasoning:** Taste and adjust the seasoning with salt and pepper. Stir in the lime juice if using.
    - **Remove Bay Leaves:** Discard the bay leaves before serving.
7. **Serve:**
    - **Garnish:** Ladle the soup into bowls and garnish with fresh cilantro and your choice of optional toppings such as sour cream, shredded cheese, diced avocado, and chopped green onions. Add crumbled tortilla chips for added crunch.

Tips:

- **Make Ahead:** Black bean soup can be made ahead of time and stored in the refrigerator for up to 5 days. It also freezes well for up to 3 months.
- **Spice Level:** Adjust the amount of chili powder and add hot sauce if you prefer a spicier soup.
- **Vegetarian Option:** This recipe is naturally vegetarian. For a vegan version, ensure that the broth is vegetable broth and omit dairy-based toppings.

Enjoy your Black Bean Soup as a comforting and nourishing meal that's perfect for any day of the week!

Pico de Gallo

Ingredients:

- **Tomatoes:** 4 medium, finely diced
- **Onion:** 1 small, finely chopped
- **Cilantro:** 1/4 cup, chopped (fresh cilantro is best)
- **Jalapeño:** 1, seeded and finely diced (adjust to taste for heat)
- **Lime Juice:** 2 tbsp (freshly squeezed)
- **Salt:** 1/2 tsp (or to taste)
- **Black Pepper:** 1/4 tsp (optional)

Instructions:

1. **Prepare Ingredients:**
    - **Dice Tomatoes:** Core and finely dice the tomatoes. If you prefer less liquid in your Pico de Gallo, you can remove the seeds.
    - **Chop Onion:** Finely chop the onion.
    - **Chop Cilantro:** Wash and chop the cilantro.
    - **Dice Jalapeño:** Seed and finely dice the jalapeño. Wear gloves if handling hot peppers, and be cautious not to touch your face.
2. **Combine Ingredients:**
    - **Mix Together:** In a medium bowl, combine the diced tomatoes, chopped onion, chopped cilantro, and diced jalapeño.
3. **Season:**
    - **Add Lime Juice:** Pour the lime juice over the mixture and stir to combine.
    - **Season:** Add salt and black pepper to taste. Mix well.
4. **Rest and Serve:**
    - **Let Flavors Meld:** For best results, let the Pico de Gallo sit for about 15-30 minutes before serving to allow the flavors to meld together.
    - **Serve:** Serve with tortilla chips, or use as a topping for tacos, burritos, grilled meats, or other Mexican dishes.

Tips:

- **Adjust Spice Level:** Adjust the amount of jalapeño to suit your desired level of spiciness. For a milder version, use less or omit the jalapeño.
- **Variations:** You can add other ingredients like finely chopped bell peppers, a splash of vinegar, or a pinch of sugar to tweak the flavor to your liking.
- **Storage:** Pico de Gallo is best enjoyed fresh, but it can be stored in an airtight container in the refrigerator for up to 2 days. The flavors may intensify over time.

Enjoy your fresh and flavorful Pico de Gallo with your favorite Mexican dishes or as a standalone snack with chips!

Guacamole

Ingredients:

- **Avocados:** 3 ripe avocados
- **Lime Juice:** 2 tbsp (freshly squeezed)
- **Salt:** 1/2 tsp (or to taste)
- **Garlic:** 1 clove, minced (optional)
- **Tomato:** 1 small, diced (optional, for extra flavor and color)
- **Onion:** 1/4 cup, finely chopped
- **Cilantro:** 1/4 cup, chopped
- **Jalapeño:** 1, seeded and finely diced (optional, for heat)
- **Black Pepper:** 1/4 tsp (optional)

Instructions:

1. **Prepare Avocados:**
   - **Cut and Remove Pit:** Cut the avocados in half lengthwise, remove the pits, and scoop the flesh into a large mixing bowl.
   - **Mash Avocados:** Use a fork or a potato masher to mash the avocado to your desired consistency. You can make it as smooth or chunky as you like.
2. **Add Lime Juice and Salt:**
   - **Season:** Add lime juice and salt to the mashed avocado. Mix well to incorporate.
3. **Add Fresh Ingredients:**
   - **Add Onion:** Stir in the finely chopped onion.
   - **Add Tomato:** If using, add the diced tomato.
   - **Add Cilantro:** Stir in the chopped cilantro.
   - **Add Jalapeño:** If you like it spicy, add the finely diced jalapeño. Adjust the amount to taste.
   - **Add Garlic and Black Pepper:** Add minced garlic and black pepper if using.
4. **Mix and Taste:**
   - **Combine Ingredients:** Mix all ingredients together until evenly distributed. Taste and adjust seasoning as needed, adding more lime juice, salt, or jalapeño if desired.
5. **Serve:**
   - **Enjoy Fresh:** Serve immediately with tortilla chips or as a topping for your favorite dishes. Guacamole is best enjoyed fresh, but you can store it in the refrigerator.

Tips:

- **Prevent Browning:** To help prevent the guacamole from browning, press a piece of plastic wrap directly onto the surface of the guacamole before refrigerating.
- **Adjust to Taste:** Feel free to customize the guacamole by adding other ingredients like diced red bell pepper, a splash of hot sauce, or a sprinkle of cumin.
- **Make Ahead:** Guacamole can be made a few hours in advance. To keep it fresh, cover it tightly and refrigerate until ready to serve.

Enjoy your homemade Guacamole with chips, tacos, or as a delicious addition to any meal!

Chicken Mole

Ingredients:

For the Mole Sauce:

- **Dried Ancho Chiles:** 3-4, stems and seeds removed
- **Dried Pasilla Chiles:** 2-3, stems and seeds removed
- **Dried Mulato Chiles:** 2-3 (optional, for additional depth)
- **Olive Oil:** 2 tbsp
- **Onion:** 1 large, chopped
- **Garlic:** 4 cloves, minced
- **Tomato Paste:** 2 tbsp
- **Almonds:** 1/4 cup, toasted (or use peanuts)
- **Cinnamon Stick:** 1
- **Cumin:** 1 tsp
- **Oregano:** 1 tsp
- **Black Pepper:** 1/2 tsp
- **Chili Powder:** 1 tbsp
- **Cocoa Powder:** 2 tbsp (unsweetened)
- **Dark Chocolate:** 2 oz, chopped (or use semi-sweet chocolate)
- **Chicken Broth:** 2-3 cups
- **Brown Sugar:** 1-2 tbsp (to taste)
- **Salt:** To taste

For the Chicken:

- **Bone-In Chicken Thighs and Drumsticks:** 2-3 lbs, skinless
- **Salt and Pepper:** To taste
- **Olive Oil:** 2 tbsp (for searing)

Instructions:

1. **Prepare the Chiles:**
    - **Toast Chiles:** Heat a skillet over medium heat. Toast the dried chiles for about 1-2 minutes, turning frequently, until fragrant. Be careful not to burn them.
    - **Soak Chiles:** Place the toasted chiles in a bowl and cover with hot water. Let them soak for about 20 minutes until softened. Drain and discard the soaking water.
2. **Make the Mole Sauce:**
    - **Blend Chiles:** In a blender or food processor, combine the soaked chiles with a small amount of chicken broth to make a smooth paste. Set aside.

- **Cook Aromatics:** In a large pot or Dutch oven, heat olive oil over medium heat. Add the chopped onion and cook until translucent, about 5 minutes. Add minced garlic and cook for another minute.
- **Add Tomato Paste:** Stir in the tomato paste and cook for 2 minutes.
- **Combine Ingredients:** Add the chile paste, almonds, cinnamon stick, cumin, oregano, black pepper, chili powder, and cocoa powder. Cook for about 5 minutes, stirring frequently.
- **Add Chocolate and Broth:** Stir in the chopped dark chocolate and 2 cups of chicken broth. Simmer for about 10-15 minutes, allowing the chocolate to melt and the sauce to thicken. Adjust the thickness with additional chicken broth as needed.
- **Sweeten and Season:** Add brown sugar to taste and adjust seasoning with salt as needed. Remove the cinnamon stick.

3. **Prepare the Chicken:**
   - **Season Chicken:** Season the chicken thighs and drumsticks with salt and pepper.
   - **Sear Chicken:** In a large skillet or Dutch oven, heat olive oil over medium-high heat. Sear the chicken pieces on all sides until golden brown, about 5-7 minutes per side. Remove chicken and set aside.
4. **Simmer Chicken in Mole Sauce:**
   - **Combine Chicken and Sauce:** Place the seared chicken pieces back into the pot with the mole sauce.
   - **Simmer:** Cover and simmer on low heat for 30-40 minutes, or until the chicken is cooked through and tender. The internal temperature of the chicken should reach 165°F (74°C).
5. **Serve:**
   - **Garnish:** Serve the Chicken Mole with a sprinkle of sesame seeds and chopped fresh cilantro, if desired.
   - **Accompaniments:** Mole is often served with rice, warm tortillas, or Mexican-style beans.

Tips:

- **Mole Variations:** Mole can vary widely in ingredients and spiciness. Feel free to adjust the type and amount of chiles and spices according to your taste.
- **Make-Ahead:** Mole sauce can be made ahead of time and stored in the refrigerator for up to a week or frozen for up to 3 months. It often tastes even better the next day as the flavors continue to develop.
- **Sweetness and Spice:** Adjust the sweetness and spiciness of the mole sauce to suit your preference. If you like it spicier, add more chili powder or a pinch of cayenne pepper.

Enjoy your rich and flavorful Chicken Mole, a true classic of Mexican cuisine!

Vegetarian Enchiladas

Ingredients:

For the Enchiladas:

- **Corn or Flour Tortillas:** 8-10 (depending on size and how tightly you roll them)
- **Olive Oil:** 1 tbsp
- **Onion:** 1 large, chopped
- **Garlic:** 3 cloves, minced
- **Bell Peppers:** 2, chopped (any color)
- **Zucchini:** 1 medium, chopped
- **Corn Kernels:** 1 cup (fresh or frozen)
- **Black Beans:** 1 can (15 oz), drained and rinsed
- **Spinach:** 2 cups, chopped (or kale or another leafy green)
- **Cumin:** 1 tsp
- **Chili Powder:** 1 tsp
- **Oregano:** 1/2 tsp
- **Salt:** To taste
- **Black Pepper:** To taste
- **Shredded Cheese:** 2 cups (cheddar, Monterey Jack, or a blend)
- **Fresh Cilantro:** For garnish (optional)

For the Enchilada Sauce:

- **Olive Oil:** 2 tbsp
- **Onion:** 1 small, finely chopped
- **Garlic:** 2 cloves, minced
- **Tomato Paste:** 2 tbsp
- **Dried Oregano:** 1 tsp
- **Cumin:** 1 tsp
- **Chili Powder:** 2 tbsp
- **Paprika:** 1 tsp
- **Vegetable Broth:** 2 cups
- **Sugar:** 1 tsp (optional, to balance the acidity)
- **Salt:** To taste
- **Black Pepper:** To taste

Instructions:

1. **Prepare the Enchilada Sauce:**
    - **Sauté Aromatics:** In a medium saucepan, heat olive oil over medium heat. Add the finely chopped onion and cook until translucent, about 5 minutes. Add minced garlic and cook for another minute.

- **Add Tomato Paste and Spices:** Stir in the tomato paste, dried oregano, cumin, chili powder, and paprika. Cook for 1-2 minutes until fragrant.
    - **Add Broth and Simmer:** Pour in the vegetable broth, stirring to combine. Bring to a simmer and cook for 10-15 minutes, allowing the sauce to thicken slightly. Adjust seasoning with salt, pepper, and sugar if needed. Remove from heat and set aside.
2. **Prepare the Filling:**
    - **Sauté Vegetables:** In a large skillet, heat olive oil over medium heat. Add the chopped onion and cook until softened, about 5 minutes. Add minced garlic and cook for another minute.
    - **Add Vegetables:** Stir in the bell peppers, zucchini, and corn. Cook until the vegetables start to soften, about 5-7 minutes.
    - **Add Beans and Spinach:** Add the black beans and chopped spinach. Cook until the spinach is wilted and everything is well combined. Season with cumin, chili powder, oregano, salt, and black pepper. Remove from heat.
3. **Assemble the Enchiladas:**
    - **Preheat Oven:** Preheat your oven to 375°F (190°C).
    - **Prepare Baking Dish:** Lightly grease a 9x13-inch baking dish.
    - **Fill Tortillas:** Spread a small amount of the enchilada sauce on the bottom of the baking dish. Fill each tortilla with a generous amount of the vegetable mixture and a sprinkle of shredded cheese. Roll up the tortillas and place them seam-side down in the prepared baking dish.
    - **Top with Sauce and Cheese:** Pour the remaining enchilada sauce over the rolled tortillas, making sure they are well covered. Sprinkle additional shredded cheese on top.
4. **Bake:**
    - **Bake Enchiladas:** Bake in the preheated oven for 20-25 minutes, or until the cheese is melted and bubbly and the enchiladas are heated through.
5. **Garnish and Serve:**
    - **Garnish:** Let the enchiladas cool slightly before serving. Garnish with fresh cilantro if desired.
    - **Serve:** Enjoy with your favorite toppings like sour cream, avocado, or salsa.

Tips:

- **Make-Ahead:** You can prepare the enchiladas and sauce a day in advance. Assemble and refrigerate, then bake when ready to serve.
- **Frozen Vegetables:** Feel free to use frozen vegetables or whatever vegetables you have on hand.
- **Cheese Alternatives:** For a dairy-free version, use vegan cheese or omit cheese altogether.

Enjoy your delicious and satisfying Vegetarian Enchiladas!

Queso Fundido

Ingredients:

- **Mexican Cheese Blend:** 2 cups (such as Chihuahua, Oaxaca, or a mix of mozzarella and Monterey Jack if unavailable)
- **Chorizo:** 8 oz (or substitute with a plant-based chorizo for a vegetarian option)
- **Onion:** 1 small, finely chopped
- **Garlic:** 2 cloves, minced
- **Bell Pepper:** 1 small, finely chopped (optional)
- **Tomato:** 1 small, diced (optional)
- **Jalapeño:** 1, seeded and finely chopped (optional, for heat)
- **Olive Oil:** 1 tbsp
- **Fresh Cilantro:** For garnish (optional)
- **Tortilla Chips, Tortillas, or Crusty Bread:** For serving

Instructions:

1. **Prepare the Chorizo:**
   - **Cook Chorizo:** In a skillet over medium heat, cook the chorizo, breaking it up with a spoon as it cooks. Cook until browned and fully cooked through, about 5-7 minutes. Remove excess fat if necessary. Transfer the chorizo to a paper towel-lined plate to drain and set aside.
2. **Sauté Vegetables:**
   - **Cook Aromatics:** In the same skillet, add olive oil and heat over medium heat. Add the finely chopped onion and cook until translucent, about 3-4 minutes. Add minced garlic and cook for another minute.
   - **Add Optional Vegetables:** If using, add the finely chopped bell pepper, diced tomato, and jalapeño. Cook until the vegetables are softened, about 5 minutes.
3. **Combine Cheese and Chorizo:**
   - **Melt Cheese:** In an oven-safe dish or a cast-iron skillet, layer the shredded cheese evenly. Top with the cooked chorizo and sautéed vegetables.
   - **Heat:** Place the dish under the broiler (or in a preheated oven at 375°F/190°C) for 5-7 minutes, or until the cheese is melted, bubbly, and slightly golden on top. Keep an eye on it to prevent burning.
4. **Garnish and Serve:**
   - **Garnish:** Remove from the oven and sprinkle with chopped fresh cilantro if desired.
   - **Serve:** Serve immediately with tortilla chips, warm tortillas, or crusty bread for dipping.

Tips:

- **Cheese Selection:** Use a good melting cheese like Chihuahua or Oaxaca for the best texture. If these are not available, a combination of mozzarella and Monterey Jack works well.
- **Add-Ins:** Feel free to customize your Queso Fundido with additional ingredients such as mushrooms, cooked peppers, or even a sprinkle of smoked paprika for extra flavor.
- **Serve Hot:** Queso Fundido is best enjoyed immediately while the cheese is still gooey and hot.

Enjoy your cheesy, savory Queso Fundido with your favorite dipping accompaniments!

Mexican Pizza

Ingredients:

For the Pizza:

- **Pizza Dough:** 1 pound (store-bought or homemade)
- **Olive Oil:** 2 tbsp (for brushing)
- **Ground Beef or Turkey:** 1/2 pound (or use a plant-based substitute for a vegetarian version)
- **Taco Seasoning:** 1 packet (or 2 tbsp homemade seasoning blend)
- **Refried Beans:** 1 cup (black or pinto beans)
- **Shredded Cheese:** 1-1.5 cups (cheddar, Monterey Jack, or a Mexican cheese blend)
- **Tortilla Chips:** Crushed (for topping)
- **Sour Cream:** For drizzling (optional)
- **Fresh Cilantro:** For garnish (optional)

For the Toppings:

- **Shredded Lettuce:** 1 cup
- **Diced Tomatoes:** 1 cup
- **Sliced Black Olives:** 1/4 cup
- **Sliced Jalapeños:** 1/4 cup (optional, for heat)
- **Chopped Green Onions:** 1/4 cup

Instructions:

1. **Preheat Oven:**
   - **Heat Oven:** Preheat your oven to 425°F (220°C). If using a pizza stone, place it in the oven to preheat as well.
2. **Prepare the Pizza Dough:**
   - **Roll Out Dough:** On a floured surface, roll out the pizza dough into a 12-inch circle or to your desired shape and thickness. Transfer the dough to a parchment-lined baking sheet or a pizza stone if using.
3. **Pre-Bake the Crust:**
   - **Brush with Oil:** Brush the pizza dough lightly with olive oil to prevent sogginess.
   - **Pre-Bake:** Bake in the preheated oven for 5-7 minutes until the crust starts to set but isn't fully cooked. Remove from the oven and set aside.
4. **Prepare the Meat:**
   - **Cook Meat:** In a skillet over medium heat, cook the ground beef or turkey until browned and cooked through. Drain any excess fat.
   - **Add Seasoning:** Add taco seasoning to the meat along with a splash of water (about 2-3 tbsp) and cook for an additional 2 minutes, stirring to combine.
5. **Assemble the Pizza:**

- **Spread Beans:** Spread a layer of refried beans evenly over the pre-baked pizza crust.
- **Add Meat:** Sprinkle the seasoned ground meat over the beans.
- **Add Cheese:** Top with shredded cheese, spreading it evenly.
6. **Bake the Pizza:**
    - **Bake:** Return the pizza to the oven and bake for an additional 8-10 minutes, or until the cheese is melted and bubbly and the crust is golden brown.
7. **Add Toppings:**
    - **Cool Slightly:** Remove the pizza from the oven and let it cool for a couple of minutes.
    - **Add Fresh Toppings:** Top with shredded lettuce, diced tomatoes, sliced black olives, sliced jalapeños, and chopped green onions. Crushed tortilla chips can be added for extra crunch.
8. **Garnish and Serve:**
    - **Garnish:** Drizzle with sour cream if desired and sprinkle with fresh cilantro.
    - **Slice and Serve:** Slice into wedges and serve immediately.

Tips:

- **Customizable:** Feel free to customize the toppings based on your preferences. You can add sliced avocado, salsa, or even a drizzle of hot sauce for extra flavor.
- **Vegetarian Option:** For a vegetarian version, use plant-based meat or add more vegetables like bell peppers and mushrooms.
- **Crispy Crust:** For an extra crispy crust, preheat your pizza stone or baking sheet before adding the dough.

Enjoy your delicious Mexican Pizza with a perfect blend of flavors and textures!

Beef Tostadas

Ingredients:

For the Beef:

- **Ground Beef:** 1 pound
- **Olive Oil:** 1 tbsp (or use vegetable oil)
- **Onion:** 1 small, finely chopped
- **Garlic:** 2 cloves, minced
- **Bell Pepper:** 1 small, finely chopped (optional)
- **Taco Seasoning:** 1 packet (or 2 tbsp homemade taco seasoning)
- **Tomato Paste:** 2 tbsp
- **Water:** 1/4 cup (or beef broth for more flavor)
- **Salt:** To taste
- **Black Pepper:** To taste

For the Tostadas:

- **Tostada Shells:** 8 (store-bought or homemade)
- **Refried Beans:** 1 cup (black or pinto beans)
- **Shredded Lettuce:** 2 cups
- **Diced Tomatoes:** 1 cup
- **Sliced Black Olives:** 1/4 cup
- **Sliced Jalapeños:** 1/4 cup (optional, for heat)
- **Shredded Cheese:** 1 cup (cheddar, Monterey Jack, or a Mexican cheese blend)
- **Sour Cream:** For drizzling (optional)
- **Fresh Cilantro:** For garnish (optional)
- **Lime Wedges:** For serving (optional)

Instructions:

1. **Prepare the Beef:**
    - **Cook Beef:** In a large skillet, heat olive oil over medium heat. Add the finely chopped onion and cook until translucent, about 3-4 minutes. Add minced garlic and cook for another minute.
    - **Add Bell Pepper:** If using, add the bell pepper and cook for another 2-3 minutes until softened.
    - **Brown Beef:** Add the ground beef to the skillet. Cook, breaking it up with a spoon, until browned and fully cooked, about 5-7 minutes.
    - **Season Beef:** Stir in the taco seasoning and tomato paste. Cook for 2 minutes to allow the flavors to combine.

- **Add Liquid:** Pour in the water (or beef broth) and stir to combine. Simmer for 5 minutes, or until the mixture thickens. Season with salt and pepper to taste. Remove from heat.
2. **Prepare Tostada Shells:**
    - **Crisp Shells:** If making tostada shells from scratch, preheat your oven to 400°F (200°C). Brush both sides of tortillas with a little oil and place them on a baking sheet. Bake for 5-7 minutes on each side, or until crispy and golden. Let cool before using.
    - **Use Store-Bought:** If using store-bought tostada shells, simply arrange them on a serving platter.
3. **Assemble the Tostadas:**
    - **Spread Beans:** Spread a layer of refried beans on each tostada shell.
    - **Add Beef:** Top with a generous amount of the seasoned beef mixture.
    - **Add Fresh Toppings:** Add shredded lettuce, diced tomatoes, sliced black olives, and sliced jalapeños if using. Sprinkle with shredded cheese.
4. **Garnish and Serve:**
    - **Garnish:** Drizzle with sour cream if desired and sprinkle with fresh cilantro.
    - **Serve:** Serve with lime wedges on the side for a fresh squeeze of lime juice.

Tips:

- **Customization:** Feel free to add or substitute toppings according to your preferences, such as avocado slices, salsa, or hot sauce.
- **Vegetarian Option:** For a vegetarian version, use seasoned black beans or a plant-based meat substitute.
- **Make-Ahead:** You can prepare the beef mixture ahead of time and store it in the refrigerator. Reheat before assembling the tostadas.

Enjoy your delicious Beef Tostadas, a crispy and flavorful meal that's sure to satisfy!

Chicken Taquitos

Ingredients:

For the Chicken Filling:

- **Boneless, Skinless Chicken Breasts or Thighs:** 1 pound
- **Olive Oil:** 1 tbsp
- **Onion:** 1 small, finely chopped
- **Garlic:** 2 cloves, minced
- **Cumin:** 1 tsp
- **Chili Powder:** 1 tsp
- **Paprika:** 1/2 tsp
- **Oregano:** 1/2 tsp
- **Salt:** To taste
- **Black Pepper:** To taste
- **Chicken Broth:** 1/2 cup
- **Shredded Cheese:** 1/2 cup (cheddar, Monterey Jack, or a Mexican blend)
- **Fresh Cilantro:** Chopped (for garnish, optional)

For the Taquitos:

- **Small Flour or Corn Tortillas:** 12 (about 6-inch diameter)
- **Vegetable Oil:** For frying

For Serving:

- **Sour Cream:** For dipping
- **Salsa:** For dipping
- **Guacamole:** For dipping
- **Shredded Lettuce:** Optional
- **Diced Tomatoes:** Optional

Instructions:

1. **Prepare the Chicken Filling:**
    - **Cook Chicken:** In a large skillet, heat olive oil over medium heat. Add the chicken breasts or thighs and cook until browned on both sides and cooked through, about 6-7 minutes per side. Remove from skillet and let rest for a few minutes.
    - **Shred Chicken:** Once cool enough to handle, shred the chicken using two forks or chop into small pieces.

- **Sauté Aromatics:** In the same skillet, add a little more olive oil if needed. Sauté the finely chopped onion until translucent, about 3-4 minutes. Add minced garlic and cook for another minute.
- **Add Spices:** Stir in cumin, chili powder, paprika, oregano, salt, and black pepper. Cook for 1 minute to allow the spices to release their flavors.
- **Combine Chicken:** Return the shredded chicken to the skillet and add chicken broth. Stir to combine and cook for an additional 5 minutes, allowing the flavors to meld and the liquid to reduce. Stir in shredded cheese until melted and well combined. Remove from heat.

2. **Assemble the Taquitos:**
   - **Prepare Tortillas:** Warm the tortillas slightly to make them more pliable. You can do this by heating them in a dry skillet over medium heat for about 30 seconds per side or wrapping them in a damp paper towel and microwaving for 30 seconds.
   - **Fill Tortillas:** Spoon about 2 tablespoons of the chicken mixture onto each tortilla. Roll the tortillas tightly around the filling and secure with a toothpick if needed.

3. **Fry the Taquitos:**
   - **Heat Oil:** In a large skillet or frying pan, heat about 1/2 inch of vegetable oil over medium heat.
   - **Fry Taquitos:** Fry the taquitos in batches, turning occasionally, until golden brown and crispy on all sides, about 3-4 minutes per side. Remove with a slotted spoon and drain on paper towels.

4. **Serve:**
   - **Garnish:** Remove toothpicks if used and garnish with chopped fresh cilantro if desired.
   - **Dipping Sauces:** Serve with sour cream, salsa, and guacamole for dipping. Optionally, add shredded lettuce and diced tomatoes for extra freshness.

Tips:

- **Oven-Baked Taquitos:** For a healthier version, you can bake the taquitos. Preheat your oven to 425°F (220°C), place the taquitos on a baking sheet lined with parchment paper, and brush them lightly with oil. Bake for 15-20 minutes, or until crispy and golden brown, turning halfway through.
- **Freezing:** You can freeze taquitos before frying. Assemble and roll them, then place on a baking sheet and freeze until solid. Transfer to a freezer bag and store for up to 3 months. Fry from frozen, adding a couple of extra minutes to the cooking time.
- **Variations:** Feel free to customize the filling by adding ingredients such as diced green chilies, chopped black olives, or sautéed bell peppers.

Enjoy your crispy and delicious Chicken Taquitos with all your favorite toppings and dips!

Tex-Mex Chicken Salad

Ingredients:

For the Salad:

- **Cooked Chicken Breast:** 2 cups, diced (grilled or roasted)
- **Romaine Lettuce:** 4 cups, chopped
- **Cherry Tomatoes:** 1 cup, halved
- **Black Beans:** 1 can (15 oz), drained and rinsed
- **Corn Kernels:** 1 cup (fresh, frozen, or canned)
- **Red Bell Pepper:** 1, diced
- **Avocado:** 1, diced
- **Shredded Cheese:** 1 cup (cheddar or a Mexican cheese blend)
- **Tortilla Chips:** Crushed, for topping
- **Cilantro:** Chopped, for garnish (optional)

For the Dressing:

- **Greek Yogurt or Sour Cream:** 1/2 cup
- **Mayonnaise:** 1/4 cup
- **Lime Juice:** 2 tbsp (about 1 lime)
- **Chili Powder:** 1 tsp
- **Cumin:** 1/2 tsp
- **Garlic Powder:** 1/2 tsp
- **Salt:** To taste
- **Black Pepper:** To taste
- **Hot Sauce:** A few dashes (optional, for extra kick)

Instructions:

1. **Prepare the Salad:**
    - **Combine Ingredients:** In a large salad bowl, combine the chopped romaine lettuce, diced chicken breast, cherry tomatoes, black beans, corn kernels, red bell pepper, and diced avocado.
    - **Add Cheese:** Sprinkle the shredded cheese over the salad.
2. **Prepare the Dressing:**
    - **Mix Dressing:** In a small bowl, whisk together the Greek yogurt (or sour cream), mayonnaise, lime juice, chili powder, cumin, garlic powder, salt, black pepper, and hot sauce if using. Adjust seasoning to taste.
3. **Assemble the Salad:**
    - **Dress Salad:** Drizzle the dressing over the salad and toss gently to combine, making sure all ingredients are coated.

- **Top with Chips:** Just before serving, sprinkle crushed tortilla chips over the top for added crunch.
4. **Garnish and Serve:**
   - **Garnish:** Garnish with chopped cilantro if desired.
   - **Serve:** Serve immediately or chill for up to an hour before serving.

Tips:

- **Grilled Chicken:** For extra flavor, marinate the chicken in a Tex-Mex seasoning blend before grilling or roasting.
- **Customizations:** Add other Tex-Mex ingredients such as sliced jalapeños, diced red onions, or pickled vegetables for more variety.
- **Vegetarian Option:** For a vegetarian version, replace the chicken with extra beans or grilled vegetables.

Enjoy your vibrant and delicious Tex-Mex Chicken Salad! It's a perfect combination of fresh ingredients with a flavorful twist.

Mexican Stuffed Shells

Ingredients:

For the Stuffed Shells:

- **Jumbo Pasta Shells:** 20-24 shells
- **Ground Beef or Turkey:** 1 pound (or a plant-based substitute)
- **Taco Seasoning:** 1 packet (or 2 tbsp homemade taco seasoning)
- **Cream Cheese:** 4 oz, softened
- **Shredded Cheddar Cheese:** 1 cup
- **Shredded Monterey Jack Cheese:** 1 cup
- **Chopped Green Onions:** 1/4 cup
- **Chopped Cilantro:** 1/4 cup
- **Black Beans:** 1 cup, drained and rinsed
- **Corn Kernels:** 1/2 cup (fresh, frozen, or canned)

For the Sauce:

- **Enchilada Sauce:** 1 can (15 oz) or homemade
- **Sour Cream:** 1/2 cup (optional, for creaminess)
- **Diced Tomatoes:** 1 cup (optional, for extra flavor)

For Garnish (optional):

- **Sliced Jalapeños:** For a bit of heat
- **Chopped Fresh Cilantro:** For garnish
- **Sour Cream:** For serving
- **Sliced Avocado:** For a fresh touch

Instructions:

1. **Cook the Pasta Shells:**
   - **Boil Shells:** Cook the jumbo pasta shells according to package instructions until al dente. Drain and let cool slightly.
2. **Prepare the Filling:**
   - **Cook Meat:** In a large skillet over medium heat, cook the ground beef or turkey until browned and cooked through. Drain any excess fat.
   - **Add Seasoning:** Stir in the taco seasoning and cook for another 2 minutes. If the mixture is too dry, add a splash of water or beef broth.
   - **Mix Cheese and Beans:** In a bowl, combine the cream cheese, shredded cheddar cheese, shredded Monterey Jack cheese, chopped green onions, chopped cilantro, black beans, and corn. Mix well.

- **Combine:** Stir the cooked ground meat into the cheese mixture until well combined.
3. **Assemble the Shells:**
   - **Stuff Shells:** Preheat your oven to 375°F (190°C). Spread a thin layer of enchilada sauce on the bottom of a baking dish.
   - **Fill Shells:** Stuff each cooked pasta shell with the meat and cheese mixture and place them in the prepared baking dish.
   - **Add Sauce:** Pour the remaining enchilada sauce over the stuffed shells. If desired, mix sour cream into the enchilada sauce for extra creaminess.
4. **Bake:**
   - **Bake:** Cover with aluminum foil and bake in the preheated oven for 25-30 minutes. Remove the foil and bake for an additional 5-10 minutes, or until the sauce is bubbly and the cheese is melted and slightly golden.
5. **Garnish and Serve:**
   - **Garnish:** Garnish with sliced jalapeños, chopped fresh cilantro, and a dollop of sour cream. Add sliced avocado if desired.
   - **Serve:** Serve hot and enjoy with additional toppings or sides like Mexican rice or a simple green salad.

Tips:

- **Customization:** Feel free to customize the filling with other ingredients like diced bell peppers, sautéed mushrooms, or chopped green chilies.
- **Vegetarian Option:** For a vegetarian version, use black beans or lentils instead of meat, and add extra veggies to the filling.
- **Make-Ahead:** You can prepare the stuffed shells ahead of time and store them in the refrigerator before baking. Just add a few extra minutes to the baking time if cooking from cold.

Enjoy your hearty and flavorful Mexican Stuffed Shells, a wonderful blend of Italian and Mexican cuisine!

Pork and Pineapple Tacos

Ingredients:

For the Pork:

- **Pork Shoulder (or Pork Tenderloin):** 1.5 pounds, cut into small cubes
- **Olive Oil:** 2 tbsp
- **Onion:** 1 medium, finely chopped
- **Garlic:** 3 cloves, minced
- **Ground Cumin:** 1 tsp
- **Paprika:** 1 tsp
- **Chili Powder:** 1 tsp
- **Oregano:** 1/2 tsp
- **Salt:** To taste
- **Black Pepper:** To taste
- **Pineapple Juice:** 1/2 cup
- **Soy Sauce:** 2 tbsp
- **Lime Juice:** 2 tbsp
- **Brown Sugar:** 1 tbsp (optional, for added sweetness)
- **Fresh Pineapple:** 1 cup, diced (for added texture and flavor)

For the Tacos:

- **Small Corn or Flour Tortillas:** 8-10
- **Shredded Cabbage:** 2 cups
- **Chopped Fresh Cilantro:** 1/4 cup
- **Sliced Radishes:** 1/2 cup
- **Diced Red Onion:** 1/4 cup
- **Lime Wedges:** For serving

For the Salsa (optional):

- **Tomatoes:** 2 medium, diced
- **Red Onion:** 1/4 cup, finely chopped
- **Cilantro:** 2 tbsp, chopped
- **Jalapeño:** 1 small, seeded and minced
- **Lime Juice:** 1 tbsp
- **Salt:** To taste

Instructions:

1. **Prepare the Pork:**

- **Cook Pork:** Heat olive oil in a large skillet over medium-high heat. Add the pork cubes and cook until browned on all sides, about 5-7 minutes.
- **Add Aromatics:** Add the chopped onion and cook until softened, about 3 minutes. Stir in minced garlic and cook for an additional minute.
- **Season and Simmer:** Add cumin, paprika, chili powder, oregano, salt, and black pepper. Stir to combine. Pour in pineapple juice, soy sauce, lime juice, and brown sugar if using. Bring to a simmer.
- **Simmer:** Reduce heat to low and cover. Simmer for 30-40 minutes, or until the pork is tender and the sauce has thickened. Stir occasionally. Add diced pineapple during the last 10 minutes of cooking.

2. **Prepare the Tacos:**
   - **Warm Tortillas:** Warm the tortillas in a dry skillet over medium heat or wrap them in a damp paper towel and microwave for 30 seconds until pliable.
   - **Assemble Tacos:** Fill each tortilla with a portion of the pork mixture.
3. **Prepare the Salsa (optional):**
   - **Mix Salsa Ingredients:** In a small bowl, combine diced tomatoes, red onion, cilantro, jalapeño, lime juice, and salt. Mix well and set aside.
4. **Garnish and Serve:**
   - **Add Toppings:** Top the tacos with shredded cabbage, chopped cilantro, sliced radishes, and diced red onion. Add a spoonful of salsa if desired.
   - **Serve:** Serve with lime wedges for squeezing over the tacos.

Tips:

- **Customize:** Feel free to adjust the spice level by adding more chili powder or including extra jalapeños.
- **Make Ahead:** You can prepare the pork mixture a day in advance and store it in the refrigerator. Reheat before assembling the tacos.
- **Vegetarian Option:** Substitute the pork with sautéed mushrooms or a plant-based protein and follow the same cooking method.

Enjoy your flavorful and refreshing Pork and Pineapple Tacos! They offer a delightful combination of sweet, savory, and tangy flavors that are sure to please.

Chili Verde

Ingredients:

For the Chili Verde:

- **Pork Shoulder (or Pork Butt):** 2 pounds, cut into 1-inch cubes
- **Olive Oil:** 2 tbsp
- **Onion:** 1 large, finely chopped
- **Garlic:** 4 cloves, minced
- **Green Chiles:** 2 cups, diced (can use a mix of roasted and canned green chiles; such as Hatch or Anaheim peppers)
- **Tomatillos:** 4-5 medium, husked and diced (or use 1 can of diced tomatillos, drained)
- **Chicken Broth:** 4 cups
- **Cumin:** 1 tsp
- **Oregano:** 1/2 tsp
- **Ground Coriander:** 1/2 tsp
- **Bay Leaves:** 2
- **Salt:** To taste
- **Black Pepper:** To taste
- **Lime Juice:** 2 tbsp
- **Fresh Cilantro:** 1/4 cup, chopped (for garnish)

For Serving:

- **Rice:** Steamed white or brown rice
- **Warm Tortillas:** Flour or corn tortillas
- **Shredded Cheese:** Optional, for topping
- **Sour Cream:** Optional, for topping

Instructions:

1. **Prepare the Pork:**
   - **Sear Pork:** Heat olive oil in a large pot or Dutch oven over medium-high heat. Add the pork cubes in batches, searing them on all sides until browned. Remove pork and set aside.
2. **Cook the Base:**
   - **Sauté Aromatics:** In the same pot, add a bit more oil if needed. Sauté the chopped onion until translucent, about 5 minutes. Add minced garlic and cook for an additional minute.
3. **Combine Ingredients:**
   - **Add Chiles and Tomatillos:** Stir in the diced green chiles and tomatillos, cooking for another 5 minutes.

- **Add Pork and Broth:** Return the seared pork to the pot. Pour in the chicken broth. Stir in cumin, oregano, ground coriander, bay leaves, salt, and black pepper.

4. **Simmer:**
   - **Cook:** Bring the mixture to a boil, then reduce heat to low. Cover and simmer for 1.5 to 2 hours, or until the pork is tender and the flavors have melded together. Stir occasionally.
5. **Finish and Serve:**
   - **Adjust Seasoning:** Remove the bay leaves. Stir in lime juice and adjust seasoning with additional salt and pepper if needed.
   - **Garnish:** Garnish with chopped fresh cilantro.
6. **Serve:**
   - **Accompaniments:** Serve the Chili Verde hot with steamed rice and warm tortillas. Top with shredded cheese and sour cream if desired.

Tips:

- **Tomatillos:** If fresh tomatillos are unavailable, you can use canned diced tomatillos. For a smoother texture, blend the tomatillos and green chiles before adding them to the pot.
- **Heat Level:** Adjust the amount of green chiles based on your preferred heat level. If you like it spicier, use hotter varieties of chiles.
- **Make-Ahead:** Chili Verde can be made ahead of time and stored in the refrigerator for up to 3 days or frozen for up to 3 months. Reheat thoroughly before serving.

Enjoy your flavorful and comforting Chili Verde! It's a satisfying dish with a unique twist that's sure to warm you up.

Chicken and Spinach Enchiladas

Ingredients:

For the Enchiladas:

- **Cooked Chicken Breast:** 2 cups, shredded (you can use rotisserie chicken or cooked chicken breasts)
- **Fresh Spinach:** 3 cups, chopped
- **Olive Oil:** 1 tbsp
- **Onion:** 1 small, finely chopped
- **Garlic:** 2 cloves, minced
- **Cream Cheese:** 4 oz, softened
- **Shredded Monterey Jack Cheese:** 1 cup
- **Shredded Cheddar Cheese:** 1 cup
- **Tortillas:** 8-10 (corn or flour)
- **Enchilada Sauce:** 2 cups (store-bought or homemade)
- **Salt:** To taste
- **Black Pepper:** To taste

For the Garnish:

- **Chopped Fresh Cilantro:** For garnish
- **Sour Cream:** For serving
- **Sliced Jalapeños:** For a bit of heat (optional)
- **Diced Red Onion:** For a fresh crunch (optional)
- **Lime Wedges:** For serving

Instructions:

1. **Prepare the Filling:**
   - **Cook Spinach:** Heat olive oil in a large skillet over medium heat. Add the chopped onion and cook until translucent, about 3-4 minutes. Add minced garlic and cook for another minute.
   - **Add Spinach:** Stir in the chopped spinach and cook until wilted, about 2 minutes. Remove from heat.
   - **Combine Ingredients:** In a large bowl, combine shredded chicken, the spinach mixture, softened cream cheese, 1 cup of shredded Monterey Jack cheese, salt, and black pepper. Mix well.
2. **Assemble the Enchiladas:**
   - **Preheat Oven:** Preheat your oven to 375°F (190°C).
   - **Warm Tortillas:** Warm the tortillas in a dry skillet over medium heat or microwave them for 30 seconds to make them more pliable.

- **Fill Tortillas:** Spoon about 2-3 tablespoons of the chicken and spinach mixture onto each tortilla. Roll up the tortillas and place them seam-side down in a baking dish.
- **Add Sauce:** Pour the enchilada sauce evenly over the rolled tortillas.

3. **Bake:**
   - **Top with Cheese:** Sprinkle the remaining shredded Monterey Jack cheese and shredded cheddar cheese over the top of the enchiladas.
   - **Bake:** Cover with aluminum foil and bake in the preheated oven for 20-25 minutes. Remove the foil and bake for an additional 10 minutes, or until the cheese is melted and bubbly.
4. **Garnish and Serve:**
   - **Garnish:** Let the enchiladas cool for a few minutes before serving. Garnish with chopped fresh cilantro.
   - **Serve:** Serve with sour cream, sliced jalapeños, diced red onion, and lime wedges on the side.

Tips:

- **Make-Ahead:** You can assemble the enchiladas a day in advance and store them in the refrigerator. Add a few extra minutes to the baking time if baking from cold.
- **Vegetarian Option:** For a vegetarian version, omit the chicken and use extra spinach or other vegetables like mushrooms and bell peppers.
- **Sauce Variations:** Try using different types of enchilada sauce, such as green or spicy, to customize the flavor.

Enjoy your delicious and comforting Chicken and Spinach Enchiladas, a perfect blend of savory chicken, creamy cheese, and nutritious spinach!

Shrimp Tacos with Cilantro Lime Sauce

Ingredients:

For the Shrimp:

- **Shrimp:** 1 pound, peeled and deveined
- **Olive Oil:** 2 tbsp
- **Garlic:** 3 cloves, minced
- **Ground Cumin:** 1/2 tsp
- **Paprika:** 1/2 tsp
- **Chili Powder:** 1/2 tsp
- **Cayenne Pepper:** 1/4 tsp (optional, for extra heat)
- **Salt:** To taste
- **Black Pepper:** To taste
- **Lime Juice:** 2 tbsp (about 1 lime)

For the Cilantro Lime Sauce:

- **Sour Cream:** 1/2 cup
- **Mayonnaise:** 1/4 cup
- **Fresh Cilantro:** 1/4 cup, chopped
- **Lime Juice:** 2 tbsp (about 1 lime)
- **Garlic Powder:** 1/2 tsp
- **Salt:** To taste
- **Black Pepper:** To taste

For the Slaw:

- **Shredded Cabbage:** 2 cups (green, red, or a mix)
- **Carrot:** 1 large, grated
- **Red Onion:** 1/4 cup, thinly sliced
- **Fresh Cilantro:** 2 tbsp, chopped
- **Lime Juice:** 1 tbsp
- **Olive Oil:** 1 tbsp
- **Salt:** To taste
- **Black Pepper:** To taste

For Serving:

- **Small Corn or Flour Tortillas:** 8-10
- **Lime Wedges:** For serving
- **Extra Cilantro:** For garnish
- **Sliced Jalapeños:** For extra heat (optional)

Instructions:

1. **Prepare the Shrimp:**
     - **Season Shrimp:** In a bowl, toss the shrimp with olive oil, minced garlic, ground cumin, paprika, chili powder, cayenne pepper (if using), salt, and black pepper.
     - **Cook Shrimp:** Heat a large skillet over medium-high heat. Add the seasoned shrimp and cook for 2-3 minutes per side, or until they are pink and opaque. Remove from heat and squeeze lime juice over the shrimp.
2. **Make the Cilantro Lime Sauce:**
     - **Mix Ingredients:** In a small bowl, combine sour cream, mayonnaise, chopped cilantro, lime juice, garlic powder, salt, and black pepper. Mix well until smooth. Adjust seasoning to taste.
3. **Prepare the Slaw:**
     - **Combine Ingredients:** In a large bowl, mix shredded cabbage, grated carrot, sliced red onion, and chopped cilantro.
     - **Dress Slaw:** In a small bowl, whisk together lime juice, olive oil, salt, and black pepper. Pour the dressing over the slaw and toss to combine. Let it sit for a few minutes to let the flavors meld.
4. **Assemble the Tacos:**
     - **Warm Tortillas:** Warm the tortillas in a dry skillet over medium heat or wrap them in a damp paper towel and microwave for 30 seconds until pliable.
     - **Fill Tortillas:** Place a few shrimp in each tortilla, top with slaw, and drizzle with cilantro lime sauce.
5. **Garnish and Serve:**
     - **Garnish:** Garnish the tacos with extra cilantro and sliced jalapeños if desired. Serve with lime wedges on the side for extra zing.

Tips:

- **Shrimp Size:** Use medium to large shrimp for the best texture in tacos.
- **Sauce Variations:** For a spicier sauce, add a dash of hot sauce or a pinch of cayenne pepper.
- **Slaw Variations:** You can add other vegetables to the slaw, like bell peppers or radishes, for extra crunch and flavor.

Enjoy your delicious Shrimp Tacos with Cilantro Lime Sauce! They're a perfect combination of fresh, tangy, and flavorful ingredients that are sure to be a hit.

Bacon-Wrapped Jalapeno Poppers

Ingredients:

- **Jalapeño Peppers:** 12-15, halved and seeded
- **Cream Cheese:** 8 oz, softened
- **Shredded Cheddar Cheese:** 1 cup
- **Garlic Powder:** 1/2 tsp
- **Onion Powder:** 1/2 tsp
- **Smoked Paprika:** 1/2 tsp (optional, for added smokiness)
- **Salt:** To taste
- **Black Pepper:** To taste
- **Bacon:** 12-15 slices (one per jalapeño half)
- **Chopped Fresh Cilantro:** For garnish (optional)

Instructions:

1. **Prepare the Jalapeños:**
   - **Preheat Oven:** Preheat your oven to 400°F (200°C).
   - **Cut and Seed:** Slice the jalapeños in half lengthwise and remove the seeds and membranes (be cautious and consider wearing gloves to avoid irritation).
2. **Prepare the Filling:**
   - **Mix Cheese Filling:** In a medium bowl, combine the softened cream cheese, shredded cheddar cheese, garlic powder, onion powder, smoked paprika (if using), salt, and black pepper. Mix until well combined.
3. **Stuff the Jalapeños:**
   - **Fill Peppers:** Spoon the cheese mixture into each jalapeño half, pressing down gently to pack the filling.
4. **Wrap with Bacon:**
   - **Wrap Peppers:** Wrap each stuffed jalapeño half with a slice of bacon, securing it with a toothpick if necessary. Make sure the bacon is tightly wrapped around the pepper.
5. **Bake:**
   - **Place on Baking Sheet:** Arrange the bacon-wrapped jalapeños on a baking sheet lined with parchment paper or a wire rack (to allow the fat to drain).
   - **Bake:** Bake in the preheated oven for 20-25 minutes, or until the bacon is crispy and the cheese is melted and bubbly. For extra crispiness, you can broil them for an additional 2-3 minutes, watching carefully to avoid burning.
6. **Serve:**
   - **Garnish:** Remove the toothpicks (if used) and garnish with chopped fresh cilantro if desired.
   - **Serve:** Serve hot and enjoy!

Tips:

- **Bacon:** For the crispiest results, use regular-cut bacon rather than thick-cut. You can also partially cook the bacon (by baking it for 5-7 minutes) before wrapping to ensure it cooks thoroughly and crisps up nicely.
- **Spice Level:** Adjust the spice level by using more or fewer jalapeños, or by adding a bit of hot sauce to the cheese filling.
- **Make-Ahead:** You can prepare the jalapeños and filling ahead of time, then wrap with bacon and bake just before serving.

Enjoy your Bacon-Wrapped Jalapeño Poppers! They're a crowd-pleaser with a fantastic combination of heat, creaminess, and smoky bacon flavor.

Get smarter responses, upload files and images, and more.

Mexican Bean Salad

Ingredients:

For the Salad:

- **Black Beans:** 1 can (15 oz), drained and rinsed
- **Kidney Beans:** 1 can (15 oz), drained and rinsed
- **Corn:** 1 cup (fresh, frozen, or canned)
- **Red Bell Pepper:** 1, diced
- **Cherry Tomatoes:** 1 cup, halved
- **Red Onion:** 1/4 cup, finely chopped
- **Cucumber:** 1, diced
- **Avocado:** 1, diced
- **Fresh Cilantro:** 1/4 cup, chopped
- **Jalapeño:** 1 small, seeded and finely chopped (optional, for heat)

For the Dressing:

- **Olive Oil:** 3 tbsp
- **Lime Juice:** 3 tbsp (about 2 limes)
- **Honey:** 1 tbsp (or agave syrup)
- **Ground Cumin:** 1/2 tsp
- **Chili Powder:** 1/2 tsp
- **Garlic Powder:** 1/2 tsp
- **Salt:** To taste
- **Black Pepper:** To taste

Instructions:

1. **Prepare the Salad:**
   - **Combine Ingredients:** In a large bowl, combine the black beans, kidney beans, corn, diced red bell pepper, cherry tomatoes, red onion, cucumber, avocado, cilantro, and jalapeño if using.
   - **Mix Gently:** Toss the ingredients gently to combine, being careful not to mash the avocado.
2. **Make the Dressing:**
   - **Whisk Ingredients:** In a small bowl, whisk together the olive oil, lime juice, honey, ground cumin, chili powder, garlic powder, salt, and black pepper until well combined.
3. **Dress the Salad:**
   - **Add Dressing:** Pour the dressing over the bean salad and toss gently to coat all the ingredients evenly.
4. **Chill and Serve:**

- **Refrigerate:** Let the salad sit in the refrigerator for at least 30 minutes before serving to allow the flavors to meld together.
- **Serve:** Serve chilled or at room temperature.

Tips:

- **Beans:** You can use canned beans for convenience, but make sure to rinse them well to reduce sodium content and improve texture.
- **Customize:** Feel free to add other vegetables like chopped bell peppers, radishes, or shredded carrots. You can also add some crumbled feta cheese or sliced olives for extra flavor.
- **Make-Ahead:** This salad can be made a day in advance. Just wait to add the avocado until shortly before serving to prevent it from browning.

Enjoy your fresh and flavorful Mexican Bean Salad! It's a versatile and satisfying dish that's sure to be a hit.

www.ingramcontent.com/pod-product-compliance
Lightning Source LLC
LaVergne TN
LVHW081556060526
838201LV00054B/1916